Heart Renewed

12 Steps to Healing Your Mind, Body and Soul

Developed, Written and Compiled by Kevin Day, Founder & CEO of

LifeGate Freedom Recovery Ministries

Dedication

To you, the reader—

the one who longs to be free.

This book is written for the moments when life feels too heavy to carry, when the pain of the past seems louder than the hope of tomorrow. It's for the one who's tried to change, who's fallen and gotten back up again, who's still fighting to believe that healing is possible.

I wrote *Heart Renewed* for you—because I've seen the chains that bind hearts, and I've seen what happens when those chains are broken. You are not alone in this journey. Every word on these pages was prayed over and crafted with a desire for your freedom, your restoration, and your renewal.

May you find here the courage to face your truth, the grace to forgive yourself, and the strength to rise again. My prayer is that as you walk through these steps, you'll encounter the One who heals all wounds and makes all things new.

This book is dedicated to **you**, the brave soul who dares to believe that change is still possible.

Your story is not over. Your heart can be renewed.

— Kevin Day
Founder, LifeGate Freedom Recovery Ministries

Acknowledgment

First and foremost, I give thanks to God—the true author of every changed heart and renewed mind. Without His grace, mercy, and relentless love, *Heart Renewed* would have never been written, and I would not have had the strength or vision to share it.

To every man and woman who has walked through the doors of LifeGate Freedom Recovery Ministries— thank you. Your courage, honesty, and hunger for freedom have been my greatest teachers. Every story of struggle and victory helped shape these pages. You reminded me that healing is real, that redemption is possible, and that no one is ever too far gone for grace.

To the LifeGate team—staff, mentors, board members, and volunteers—you are the heartbeat of this ministry. Your faithfulness behind the scenes, your willingness to serve, and your belief in what God is doing through this work continue to inspire me daily.

To my family—thank you for your patience, prayers, and unending support through late nights, early mornings, and countless rewrites. You've been my steady place and constant reminder of love's endurance.

And finally, to every reader who dares to pick up this book and open your heart—thank you. You are the reason this exists. My prayer is that as you journey through these steps, you'll discover the same renewing grace that has changed my life and so many others.

May this work be a small reflection of a great God who still restores broken hearts and renews weary souls.

— *Kevin Day*
Founder, LifeGate Freedom Recovery Ministries

Contents

Foreword

Welcome to "Heart Renewed: 12 Steps to Healing Your Mind, Body and Soul". This program was prayerfully developed to guide individuals through the time-tested principles of the 12 Steps, firmly rooted in the Word of God. While the world often views recovery as simply overcoming addiction, our vision is deeper: to help men and women find a heart truly renewed.

Don't worry, you don't have to be a Christian to change your life for the better. Let the process change you into who you really are.

Heart Renewed is built on Psalm 51:10 — 'Create in me a clean heart, O God, and renew a right spirit within me.' This cry of David reflects the heart of every person who longs for healing and new life. In this program, we seek not only to address the struggles of the past, but to cultivate a renewed spirit that walks daily in the freedom and power of Christ.

The lessons in this book are designed to be both practical and spiritual. Each step is paired with Scripture, reflection questions, and prayer, providing a pathway to healing that engages both the heart and the mind. The expanded moral inventory section allows participants to deal honestly with their past while receiving God's grace and forgiveness. The final chapters focus on discipleship, purpose, and determination, ensuring that recovery leads to a Christ-centered life.

This journey is not meant to be walked alone. Heart Renewed is best experienced in fellowship with others, in accountability, and in the context of community. It is our prayer that as you work through these steps, you will not only discover freedom from bondage, but also discover your true identity in Christ, your God-given purpose, and a renewed heart ready to serve Him.

You are about to embark on one of the most exciting, fruitful, painful, joyous, enlightening journeys you have ever been on. It will be the most worthwhile journey you have ever been on. My prayer for you is to become who you are really meant to be. You can do it. Let's get started on your new life free from the pains and problems you have been going through.

May the Lord bless you as you begin this journey of renewal.

A New Way of Life Takes Time

Recovery is not a quick event — it's a lifestyle we build one choice at a time. Think of it like learning to walk again after an injury: it feels clumsy at first, but step by step, strength and balance return. In the same way, building a new sober lifestyle takes daily effort, repeated practice, and patience with yourself.

God does the work of renewal, but He invites us into the process. Every time you choose to turn away from old habits, you're rewiring your brain and reshaping your future. Don't be discouraged if it feels slow. You are not just quitting a behavior — you are learning a whole new way of life.

This journey is about more than stopping destructive behaviors. It is about developing a healthy mind, body, and spirit—becoming the person God has always intended you to be. Remember: practice, practice, practice. Over time, the new way becomes natural, and the old ways lose their hold.

How to Use This Book

Heart Renewed is designed to be more than a study guide—it is a pathway to spiritual transformation in Christ. This book can be used in both individual study and group settings. Below are some guidelines for getting the most out of your journey:

1. Begin Each Session with Prayer – Open with the *Opening Prayer of Surrender* to set your heart and mind on Christ.

2. Follow the Lesson Order – The program is structured to build step by step. Complete lessons in sequence to ensure a strong foundation.

3. Engage With Scripture – Each lesson includes key Bible verses. Take time to read, reflect, and even memorize them. The Word of God is central to transformation.

 4. Use the Reflection Questions – Be honest and open as you answer. These are designed to help you apply God's truth to your personal life and struggles.

5. Take Time with Step Four (Moral Inventory) – This section is intentionally more in-depth. Do not rush through it. Allow God's Spirit to guide you in honest self-examination and healing.

6. Share with Accountability Partners – Heart Renewed is meant to be walked in fellowship. Be willing to share your journey with a trusted mentor, sponsor, or small group.

7. Close Each Session with Prayer – End with the *Closing Prayer of Gratitude and Commitment, asking God to seal the lessons in your heart.

8. Commit to Consistency – Transformation takes time. Aim to meet regularly (weekly is recommended) to stay on track.

9. Leaders and Facilitators – If you are leading a group, review the Leader's Guide section for tips on facilitation, discussion, and supporting participants.

10. Trust the Process – This journey is not about perfection but progress. Lean on God's grace and remember Philippians 1:6 – 'He who began a good work in you will carry it on to completion until the day of Christ Jesus.'

As you use this book, may your heart be renewed, your mind transformed, and your life anchored in Christ.

Opening Prayer of Surrender

Lord Jesus Christ,

I surrender my life and my will to You today.

I confess that on my own I am powerless,

but through You all things are possible.

Take my life, Lord, and guide my steps.

Remove from me every chain of sin and selfishness.

Teach me to walk in Your truth,

to be willing, humble, and teachable.

Fill me with Your Holy Spirit,

that I may live with purpose,

serve others with love,

and bring glory to Your name.

Today, I choose Your will over mine.

In Jesus' name, Amen.

Heart Renewed

Readiness Evaluation

Purpose

This Readiness Evaluation is designed to help participants prayerfully reflect on their willingness, openness, and readiness to begin a Christ-centered journey of recovery and discipleship. It also provides leaders with insight into areas of strength and areas that may need extra encouragement or prayer support.

Biblical Foundation

• Proverbs 9:9 (NIV) - "Instruct the wise and they will be wiser still; teach the righteous and they will add to their learning."

• Isaiah 1:19 (NIV) – "If you are willing and obedient, you will eat the good things of the land."

• 2 Corinthians 13:5 (NIV) – "Examine yourselves to see whether you are in the faith; test yourselves."

SELF-REFLECTION QUESTIONNAIRE

Instructions: Please answer honestly. Circle the number that best represents your current level of agreement.

(1 = Strongly Disagree | 2 = Disagree | 3 = Neutral | 4 = Agree | 5 = Strongly Agree)

"Add the totals for each section. Divide by 5 for your average score."

☐ **4–5:** Healthy progress — stay consistent and humble.

☐ **3:** Growth area — reflect prayerfully on what's holding you back.

☐ **1–2:** Barrier present — seek guidance and accountability for breakthrough.

WILLINGNESS *(Questions 1–5)*

1. I am willing to admit that I cannot overcome my struggles on my own.

1 — 2 — 3 — 4 — 5

2. I am willing to be honest about my past and present struggles.

1 — 2 — 3 — 4 — 5

3. I am willing to let God's Word guide my decisions.

1 — 2 — 3 — 4 — 5

4. I am willing to be held accountable by others.

1 — 2 — 3 — 4 — 5

5. I am willing to make changes in my lifestyle if necessary.

1 — 2 — 3 — 4 — 5

If your average is not above a 3, you may want to prayerfully reflect on your current level of willingness to make necessary changes.

TEACHABLE SPIRIT *(Questions 6–10)*

6. I am open to correction and instruction without becoming defensive.

1 — 2 — 3 — 4 — 5

7. I am ready to learn from scripture, even when it convicts me.

1 — 2 — 3 — 4 — 5

8. I am willing to hear feedback from mentors, leaders, or peers.

1 — 2 — 3 — 4 — 5

9. I value wisdom and recognize I do not have all the answers.

1 — 2 — 3 — 4 — 5

10. I am open to trying new ways of living that honor God.

1 — 2 — 3 — 4 — 5

If your average is not above a 3, you may want to reevaluate your willingness to be teachable.

COMMITMENT & READINESS *(Questions 11–15)*

11. I believe God has a purpose for my life beyond addiction/struggle.

1 — 2 — 3 — 4 — 5

12. I understand that this program is not a 'quick fix' but a lifelong journey.

1 — 2 — 3 — 4 — 5

13. I am prepared to invest time and energy in my recovery and growth.

1 — 2 — 3 — 4 — 5

14. I am willing to forgive others and seek forgiveness.

1 — 2 — 3 — 4 — 5

15. I am determined to see this process through, even when it becomes difficult.

1 — 2 — 3 — 4 — 5

If your average is not above a 3, you may want to take time to reflect on how fully committed you are to this process and the changes ahead.

Reflection

Your scores are a personal snapshot of your current heart posture. There are no right or wrong answers—only opportunities for growth. If any area averages below a 3, take time to reflect and pray about what may be holding you back. Healing is always possible, but it begins with honesty, openness, and a willing heart.

SHORT ANSWER REFLECTION

Please take a few moments to answer the following questions:

1. What do you hope to gain from this program?

_____

_____

2. What fears do you have about starting this journey?

_____

_____

3. In what ways do you want God to change your life?

_____

_____

4. Who are the people you are most accountable to right now?

_____

_____

5. What keeps you from being fully willing and teachable?

_____

_____

Leader's Notes

Leaders may use this section to note areas of strength, possible resistance, and areas needing prayer or mentorship. Encourage participants in areas where willingness or teachability is low.

The First Week Sober: Your Survival Guide

A practical, no-nonsense handbook for navigating the most challenging seven days of your recovery journey.

Day 1: You Just Decided to Stop

What's Happening in Your Body and Mind

- Your brain is panicking because it's used to the substance.
- You might feel anxious, restless, or even physically sick.
- Emotions are raw and unpredictable.
- Sleep will likely be difficult.
- You might question whether you can really do this.

Your Survival Strategy for Day 1

1. Change Your Environment Immediately

- Get rid of all substances in your home - pour them out, throw them away, give them to someone else.
- Delete dealer numbers from your phone right now.
- Remove paraphernalia, bottles, pipes – everything.
- *Why this matters*: You're removing the option to use in a moment of weakness.

2. Tell Someone

- Call a friend, family member, or sponsor.
- Text someone: "I'm getting sober. Day 1. I need support."
- If you have no one, call a crisis line or AA/NA hotline.
- *Why this matters*: Secrets keep you sick. Accountability keeps you alive.

3. Survive Hour by Hour

- Don't think about tomorrow, next week, or forever.
- Your only job is not to use it for the next 60 minutes.
- When that hour is up, commit to one more.
- *Why this matters*: "One day at a time" is too much on Day 1. Think in hours.

4. Physical Survival Basics

- Drink water - lots of it.
- Eat something, even if you're not hungry (crackers, soup, toast).
- If withdrawal symptoms are severe (shaking, hallucinations, seizures), go to the ER.
- *Why this matters*: Your body is detoxing. Help it along.

5. Distraction is Your Friend

- Watch TV, take a walk, clean something, play video games.
- Anything that keeps your hands and mind busy.
- Avoid triggers: people, places, situations associated with using.
- *Why this matters*: An idle mind will convince you to use.

Day 2-3: The Hardest Days

What's Happening

- Physical withdrawal peaks for many substances.
- Your brain is screaming for what it's used to.
- Sleep is still terrible.
- You might feel depressed, angry, or emotionally numb.
- Cravings come in waves.
- You're questioning everything.

Your Survival Strategy

1. Ride the Wave

- Cravings typically last 15-30 minutes, then pass.
- When a craving hits: set a timer for 20 minutes.
- During those 20 minutes: call someone, take a shower, go for a walk, do pushups.
- Tell yourself: "I just need to get through the next 20 minutes."
- *Why this matters*: Cravings are temporary. Using has permanent consequences.

2. The HALT Check

Every time you want to use, ask yourself: Am I...

- **Hungry?**
- **Angry?**
- **Lonely?**
- **Tired?**

Then address whichever applies. Often, what feels like a craving is actually one of these needs.

3. Create a New Routine

- Wake up at the same time.
- Make your bed (sounds small, but it's a win).
- Eat three meals.
- Go to bed at the same time.
- *Why this matters*: Addiction thrives in chaos. Structure is your weapon.

4. Avoid Triggers Like Your Life Depends on It (Because It Does)

- Don't go to the bar "just to hang out".
- Don't call your using friends "just to talk".
- Don't drive past your dealer's house.

- Don't test yourself - you're not ready.
- *Why this matters*: Willpower is limited. Don't waste it on unnecessary battles.

5. Find a Meeting (Even if You Don't Want To)

- AA, NA, SMART Recovery, Celebrate Recovery - pick one
- You don't have to share, just listen.
- Get phone numbers from people who have what you want
- Go every day if possible.
- *Why this matters*: You can't do this alone, and these people understand.

Day 4-5: The Danger Zone

What's Happening

- You might start feeling a little better physically.
- Your brain will tell you: "See? You're fine. You didn't have a problem."
- Or the opposite: "This is too hard. One more time won't hurt."
- Emotional withdrawal intensifies.
- You're exhausted from fighting.

Your Survival Strategy

1. Remember Your "Why"

Write down (right now) why you decided to get sober:

- What did you lose?
- Who did you hurt?
- What was your rock bottom?
- What do you want your life to look like?

Read this list every morning and every time you want to use.

2. Play the Video Forward

When you think about using, don't stop at the high. Play the whole movie:

- The guilt and shame afterward.
- The money wasted.
- The disappointment in people's eyes.
- The consequences you'll face.
- Waking up having to start over at Day 1.

Why this matters: Your brain only remembers the good parts. Force it to remember the truth.

3. Celebrate Small Wins

- You made it 4 days - that's HUGE.
- You're doing something most people can't do.
- Treat yourself (non-substance): favorite meal, new book, movie, something.
- *Why this matters*: Recovery isn't just about what you're giving up - it's about what you're gaining.

4. Physical Activity

- Walk, run, lift weights, do yoga – anything.
- Even 10 minutes helps.
- Gets endorphins flowing naturally.
- Tires you out for better sleep.
- *Why this matters*: Your brain needs to relearn how to feel good naturally.

Day 6-7: You're Building Momentum

What's Happening

- You're almost at one week - that's a major milestone.
- Physical symptoms are improving.

- You might have moments of clarity or hope.
- But you're also vulnerable to complacency.
- The "pink cloud" might appear (feeling euphoric about sobriety).

Your Survival Strategy

1. Don't Get Cocky

- One week is amazing, but you're not cured.
- Addiction is patient - it will wait for you to let your guard down.
- Keep doing what got you here.
- *Why this matters*: More people relapse from overconfidence than from struggle.

2. Start Building Your Recovery Plan

- Find a sponsor or mentor.
- Commit to 90 meetings in 90 days (if doing 12-step).
- Schedule therapy or counseling.
- Identify your support system.
- Plan how you'll handle future triggers.
- *Why this matters*: Survival mode got you through week one. Now you need a strategy for week two and beyond.

3. Make Amends to Yourself First

- Forgive yourself for what you did while using.
- Commit to treating yourself with respect.
- Start eating better, sleeping better, and taking care of yourself.
- *Why this matters*: You can't pour from an empty cup. Self-care isn't selfish in recovery.

4. Identify Your Relapse Warning Signs

Write down what happens before you typically use:

- Certain emotions (anger, loneliness, stress).
- Certain situations (conflict, celebration, boredom).
- Certain thoughts ("I deserve it," "Just once," "I can control it").

Share this list with your support person.

5. Create Your Emergency Plan

When you want to use it, you will:

1. Call _____ (name and number)
2. Go to _____ (safe place)
3. Do _____ (healthy coping activity)
4. Remember _____ (your "why")

Universal Survival Tools for Week One

The 5-Minute Rule

If you want to use it, wait 5 minutes first. During those 5 minutes:

- Call someone.
- Pray or meditate.
- Read recovery material.
- Do jumping jacks.
- Take deep breaths.
- Usually, the intensity passes.

Phone Call List

Create a list of 5 people you can call when struggling. Put it in your phone. When you want to use it, start at #1 and call until someone answers.

Gratitude Practice

Every night, write down 3 things you're grateful for that day. Even small things:

- I didn't use today.
- I ate a meal.
- Someone smiled at me.

This rewires your brain toward positivity.

The Reality Check

Keep a note in your phone or wallet with the consequences of using:

- Legal problems
- Lost relationships
- Financial cost
- Health damage
- Broken promises

Read it when tempted.

What If You Slip?

If you use during your first week:

1. **Don't give up** - a slip doesn't have to become a relapse.
2. **Tell someone immediately** - secrets will kill you.
3. **Figure out what triggered it** - what can you do differently?

4. **Start again** - Day 1 starts now.
5. **Get more support** - what you're doing isn't enough yet.

Remember: Recovery isn't about perfection. It's about progress. Many people who have years of sobriety now have had multiple Day 1's before it stuck.

The Truth About Week One

It's going to be hard. Anyone who tells you otherwise is lying.

You will want to quit. Multiple times. That's normal.

You will question if you can do this. You can. Millions of people have walked this path before you.

You will feel uncomfortable. Growth always is.

But here's what else is true:

- Every hour you stay sober, your brain is healing.
- Every day you don't use, you're proving to yourself you can do hard things.
- Every craving you survive makes you stronger.
- Every person you reach out to becomes part of your support system.
- Every small win builds momentum.

You don't have to do this perfectly. You just have to not give up.

Resources for Your First Week

24/7 Hotlines:

- SAMHSA National Helpline: 1-800-662-4357 (free, confidential, 24/7)
- Crisis Text Line: Text HOME to 741741
- AA Hotline: Check your local area
- NA Hotline: 1-800-662-4357

Find Meetings:

- AA: aa.org (in-person and online meetings)
- NA: na.org
- SMART Recovery: smartrecovery.org
- Celebrate Recovery: celebraterecovery.com

Apps:

- I Am Sober (tracks sobriety, daily motivation)
- Nomo (sobriety clock and community)
- Sober Grid (social network for recovery)
- Meeting Guide (find AA meetings near you)

Final Word

Your first week sober is about survival, not perfection. It's about making it through one more hour, one more day. It's about proving to yourself that you're stronger than your addiction.

Kevin's been sober for 42 years, and his first week looked a lot like yours. Everyone who has long-term sobriety started exactly where you are right now - scared, uncertain, fighting for their life.

You can do this.

Not because it's easy. Not because you're special. But because you're willing to fight for one more day.

And that's enough.

Introduction to Part One
Foundations of Recovery in Christ

Every building must rest on a solid foundation. In the same way, recovery and discipleship must begin with a firm spiritual foundation rooted in Christ. Before we dive into the 12 Steps, we must first understand why this journey matters, how it is anchored in God's Word, and what it means to walk as a disciple of Jesus. This section lays the groundwork for the steps that follow by addressing the purpose of this program, its biblical roots, the call to count the cost of discipleship, and the importance of fellowship and accountability. With these foundations in place, participants will be better prepared to begin the 12-step journey with Christ at the center.

The Purpose of This Journey

The Heart Renewed journey is more than recovery—it is about transformation in Christ. The 12 Steps, when rooted in Scripture, provide a pathway to healing, freedom, and discipleship. Our goal is not simply to stop destructive behaviors, but to live fully surrendered to Jesus Christ and walk in His purpose.

Key Scriptures:

• John 10:10 (NIV) – Jesus came to give life abundantly.

• 2 Corinthians 5:17 (KJV) "Therefore if any man be in Christ, he is a new creature: old things are passed away; behold, all things are become new."

REFLECTION QUESTIONS:

1. What does live abundantly in Christ mean to you?

_____

_____

_____

_____

2. How do you hope Heart Renewed will change your life?

_____

_____

_____

_____

Prayer Focus:

Ask God to reveal His purpose for your life as you begin this journey.

The Biblical Roots of the 12 Steps

The 12 Steps are not man-made wisdom, but principles that can be traced directly to the Word of God. Each step corresponds with biblical truths of repentance, confession, forgiveness, and discipleship. Understanding this foundation will help participants see the steps as a spiritual journey with Christ, not just a recovery method.

Key Scriptures:

• Psalm 51:10 (KJV) – "Create in me a clean heart, O God."

• James 5:16 (NIV) – "Confess your sins to one another and pray for each other."

REFLECTION QUESTIONS:

1. How does seeing the 12 Steps through the lens of Scripture change your perspective?

_____

_____

_____

_____

2. Which biblical truth stands out to you as most important in beginning this journey?

_____

_____

_____

_____

Prayer Focus:

Thank God for providing a biblical foundation for healing and transformation.

The Call to Discipleship – Counting the Cost

Following Jesus requires surrender, obedience, and commitment. Discipleship means counting the cost of leaving behind old ways and living a new life in Christ. Heart Renewed invites participants not just to recover from past struggles, but to take up their cross daily and follow Jesus.

Key Scriptures:

• Luke 9:23 (NIV) – Whoever wants to be my disciple must deny themselves and take up their cross daily.

• Luke 14:28 (NIV) – Count the cost before building.

REFLECTION QUESTIONS:

1. What are some things you may need to give up to follow Jesus wholeheartedly?

_____

_____

_____

_____

2. Why is it important to 'count the cost' before beginning this journey?

_____

_____

_____

_____

Prayer Focus:

Pray for strength to surrender fully and follow Jesus regardless of the cost.

The Call to Discipleship – Counting the Cost

Following Christ means more than believing—it means surrendering our lives to Him fully. Discipleship is not about convenience or comfort but about laying down our will and trusting God's plan. Jesus Himself said that anyone who would follow Him must take up their cross daily. This chapter explores the reality of what it means to count the cost and to live as a true disciple of Christ.

Surrendering All

Life has a funny way of throwing curveballs when you least expect them. You plan, you prepare, and still, things go sideways. Sound familiar? Sometimes, no matter how much we try to hold the reins, life has a way of reminding us that we're not in control. That's where the concept of surrendering all comes into play—not as a sign of weakness, but as a step toward liberation, peace, and spiritual growth.

But wait, surrender? Doesn't that mean giving up? Well, not quite. Surrendering all doesn't mean waving a white flag in defeat; it's about handing over the battles you were never meant to fight alone. It's about trusting in Someone greater than yourself to carry the load.

What Does 'Surrendering All' Really Mean?

At its core, surrendering all is about letting go—letting go of control, fear, doubt, and even the need to understand every little detail. It's about trusting God's plan, even when the road ahead looks foggy. Instead of clinging to your own limited perspective, you're choosing to believe that a higher power has your best interests at heart.

Here's what surrendering all might look like in your daily life:

• Releasing Control: Stop trying to micromanage every outcome. Leave space for God to work in unexpected ways.

• Trusting the Unknown: Faith doesn't require you to have all the answers. Let go of the need to predict or plan every step.

• Accepting Imperfections: Surrendering means embracing your flaws and trusting God to work through them.

• Giving Up Worry: Hand over your anxieties, knowing that worrying doesn't add a single moment to your life.

Surrendering all isn't a one-time event; it's a daily practice. Some days, it'll feel easier than others. And that's okay.

The Freedom Found in Letting Go

It's ironic, isn't it? The more we try to control everything, the more trapped we feel. But when we let go, we begin to experience freedom. Surrendering all can unlock a peace that surpasses understanding.

When you stop clinging to your own plans and start trusting in God's timing, you'll notice a shift:

• Peace in Chaos: Life doesn't have to be perfect for you to feel at peace. By surrendering, you trade anxiety for calm.

• Clarity in Uncertainty: Letting go of control opens the door for divine guidance and wisdom.

• Stronger Faith: The act of surrendering strengthens your relationship with God as you learn to rely on Him.

Think of it like unclenching your fists. When your hands are open, you're not just letting go—you're also ready to receive.

Steps to Begin Surrendering All

If surrendering all feels like an overwhelming concept, don't worry. It's a process, not a sprint. Start small and build from there.

• Acknowledge You're Not in Control: Recognize your limitations. You can't do it all, and that's perfectly okay.

• Pray with Intention: Be honest with God about what you're struggling to let go of.

• Practice Gratitude: Focus on what you already have. Gratitude helps you trust that God is providing for you.

• Release Daily: Each morning, make a conscious choice to let go and trust God.

• Seek Community: Surround yourself with people who encourage and remind you to surrender.

Remember, baby steps are still steps. The journey of surrendering all starts with one small act of faith.

Surrendering All in the Tough Times

Let's be real, surrendering is hardest when life feels like a storm. When the waves are crashing, and the boat feels like it's sinking, surrender might be the last thing on your mind.

But here's the truth: surrendering during tough times is when it matters most. It's in the moments of uncertainty, pain, and fear that surrender becomes an act of profound faith.

• When You're Waiting: Trust God's timing and believe that delays aren't denials.

• When You're Hurting: Surrendering invites God to work through your pain for His purpose.

• When You're Afraid: Surrendering replaces fear with trust, reminding you that you're not walking alone.

Surrendering all doesn't mean denying your emotions. It means bringing them to God and trusting Him to carry what you can't.

FAQs About Surrendering All

1. Does surrendering all mean I stop trying?

Not at all! Surrendering isn't about laziness or apathy. It's about focusing on what you can control—your attitude, actions, and faith—while letting go of what's beyond your grasp.

2. How do I know if I've truly surrendered?

True surrender brings peace, even in the midst of chaos. If you're still feeling stressed or anxious, it might be a sign to dig deeper and release more.

3. What if I take back what I've surrendered?

Hey, it happens! The important thing is to recognize it and surrender again. God's grace is big enough to cover our back-and-forth moments.

4. Can I surrender without faith in God?

While surrender is often linked to faith, the principle of letting go can benefit anyone. However, surrendering to God adds a deeper layer of trust and purpose.

5. Why does surrendering feel so hard?

Because it goes against our nature! We're wired to want control. Surrendering requires humility and trust, which can take time to develop.

Conclusion

Surrendering all isn't about giving up; it's about giving in—to peace, to freedom, to trust. It's a daily decision to loosen your grip and let God take the wheel.

Life won't always make sense, and that's okay. You don't need to have it all figured out. What matters is that you're willing to let go of what's holding you back and embrace the freedom that comes with surrendering all.

So, what's one thing you can surrender today? Trust that, as you let go, you're opening the door to a life of peace, purpose, and divine guidance. After all, the best journeys begin when we finally release the map.

Reflection & Prayer

Reflection Questions:

• What areas of your life are hardest to surrender to God?

• How does surrendering lead to freedom rather than defeat?

• What is one practical step you can take today to surrender all to Christ?

Prayer Focus:

Ask God to give you the courage to surrender every area of your life to Him daily. Pray for peace, clarity, and stronger faith as you trust Him with your future.

Walking Together in Fellowship & Accountability

God designed us to grow in community. Recovery and discipleship cannot be walked alone. Accountability, encouragement, and fellowship with other believers provide strength and support. Through Heart Renewed, the body of Christ helps us stay strong and walk faithfully.

Key Scriptures:

• Ecclesiastes 4:9–10 (NLT Paraphrased)– Two are better than one, for they help each other succeed.

• Hebrews 10:24–25 (NIV Paraphrased) – Do not neglect meeting together, but encourage one another.

REFLECTION QUESTIONS:

1. Who has God placed in your life to walk with you in this journey?

_____

_____

_____

_____

2.How can accountability strengthen your recovery and discipleship?

_____

_____

_____

_____

Prayer Focus:

Pray for God to bring trustworthy people into your life who will encourage and support your walk.

STEP 1

We admitted we were powerless over our addiction and that our lives had become unmanageable.

Scripture Foundation

"My grace is sufficient for you, for my power is made perfect in weakness." (2 Corinthians 12:9) (NIV)

"For I know that nothing good dwells in me, that is, in my flesh. For I have the desire to do what is right, but not the ability to carry it out." (Romans 7:18) (ESV)

Introduction – The Doorway to Freedom

Step 1 is the foundation of recovery. Without it, there is no progress. Admitting powerlessness is frightening—we fear it means weakness or defeat. But in truth, this admission is the doorway to freedom. The moment we confess that our lives are unmanageable is the moment we stop lying to ourselves and begin to open our hearts to God's transforming power.

Step 1 begins with honesty. It is an admission that we cannot save ourselves. We are powerless over our addictions, and the fruit of that powerlessness is the chaos and unmanageability of our lives. To take Step 1 means to stop lying to ourselves and to God. It means acknowledging: "I cannot fix myself. I cannot manage my life. I need God's help."

Teaching & Lesson Content

1. The Powerlessness We Resist

One of the hardest truths to accept in recovery is that we are powerless. Everything in us wants to deny it. We tell ourselves, "I can stop anytime I want," or "This time will be different." But if we are truly honest, we see the cycle: we use, we try to quit, we fail, and we fall back into despair.

Denial tells us that we are in control. Minimization whispers that it's "not that bad." Blame shifts responsibility onto others. But the truth of Step 1 is that our choices have led us into destruction, and no human effort alone can restore us.

The Bible makes it clear that apart from God, we cannot master sin. Romans 7:18 (NIV) says, *"For I have the desire to do what is good, but I cannot carry it out."* Admitting powerlessness is not weakness—it's the beginning of wisdom. It's saying, "I can't do this on my own, but with God, all things are possible" (Matthew 19:26) (NIV Paraphrased)

2. Unmanageability – The Evidence of Addiction

Powerlessness always shows itself in the wreckage of unmanageable lives. Addiction is not just about the substance or behavior—it's about the chaos it brings. Broken relationships, legal problems, financial struggles, health issues, spiritual emptiness: these are the signs that life is out of control.

Proverbs 14:12 (NIV) warns, *"There is a way that appears to be right, but in the end it leads to death."* Step 1 asks us to stop lying to ourselves. We must face the truth: our best thinking has led us to brokenness. Real healing begins when we stop pretending we can still manage the mess on our own.

3. The Lie of Control vs. The Gift of Surrender

Addiction whispers, "You are in control." But the truth is that our addiction controls us. The more we try to prove our control, the deeper we sink. Jesus asked in Matthew 6:27 (NIV) *"Can any of you by worrying add a single hour to your life?"* If we cannot control even the length of our lives, how much less can we control addiction without God's help?

Surrender is not giving up; it is giving over. It's handing the reins to God and admitting that He is able to do for us what we cannot do for ourselves. True strength begins with surrender.

4. The Trap of Blame

When life feels unmanageable, our instinct is to point fingers. We blame parents, friends, enemies, trauma, or circumstances. While these may explain some of our pain, they do not excuse our actions. Blame keeps us chained to the past.

Step 1 challenges us to take responsibility: "Yes, I was hurt. Yes, life has been unfair. But today, I choose to stop blaming and start changing." Galatians 6:5 (NIV) tells us, *"Each one should carry their own load."* Healing begins when we own our brokenness instead of shifting it to others.

5. Facing the Truth with Courage

Step 1 is about brutal honesty. We cannot heal what we will not face. We often minimize our addiction: "It's not that bad" or "At least I'm not like them." But denial is the enemy of freedom.

John 8:32 (NIV) declares, *"Then you will know the truth, and the truth will set you free."* Facing the truth may feel painful, but it is the doorway to peace. Recovery is not about image—it is about reality. When we confess that our lives are unmanageable, we create space for God's power to enter and bring order to the chaos.

Story Box – My Personal Journey

My personal adventure with powerlessness began long before I got sober or worked a program. My problem in life was that I was always trying to grasp control of something—anything—because deep down I knew I wasn't in control of anything. I didn't have to do a long, exhaustive study of my life to see the truth. I already knew I couldn't control my relationships, jobs, finances, feelings of self-worth, or even the humiliation I felt every day when I failed to make the right decisions. Every wrong choice screamed at me: "You're powerless." The more I fought to control some areas of my life, the more it spun out of control. My life was an endless circle of self-destructive behaviors, and I didn't even understand why I kept sabotaging myself with terrible decisions. Over and over, I asked, "Why is this happening to me?" The truth was, I was powerless. But I haven't seen it yet. To me, admitting powerlessness felt like giving up. Everything I had grown up believing told me that surrender meant weakness. It felt like being torn down to the very core of who I was—like when I first entered the military and the Air Force stripped me of everything I thought I knew. The only difference was, in the service there was hope of being built back up again. In my addiction, I couldn't see any hope at all. When I first began looking at Step 1, I thought my problem was only with drugs and alcohol. I didn't want to admit that my whole life had become unmanageable. But the truth was written all over my past. I lost jobs, ruined relationships, and broken trust with nearly everyone close to me. My addiction had led me into legal trouble that could have cost me a life sentence. Every promise I made—to myself or to others—was broken the moment temptation came back around. For years, I told myself it wasn't that bad. I blamed circumstances. I blamed people. I minimized the damage. But when my sponsor helped me hold my life up to the light of truth, I saw clearly: it wasn't just about getting high, it was about a life that I could no longer manage on my own. For me, it would have been easy to avoid working the 12 steps because I had such a radical encounter with God in that jail cell. But I thank Him that I still got involved in the process of renewing my mind and actions through the steps. When I sat down with a sponsor, I saw how unmanageable my life really was. On my own, I had minimized and lied to myself about the damage I caused. I also blamed others for many of my problems, but in reality, it was my own choices that had led me there. When my life was finally held up to scrutiny, I could no longer deny it.

That was the beginning of freedom for me. Once I admitted my life was unmanageable, God could begin to rebuild it. What I once thought was the end of everything became the start of a new way of living. That was the moment I truly began to accept the process of recovery.

But Step 1 was the beginning of that hope. It taught me that being powerless wasn't the end—it was the starting place where God could finally rebuild me.

Worksheet: Facing Unmanageability

Step 1 Practical Guide – Facing Powerlessness and Unmanageability

1. **Write Your Addiction History** – List the substances or behaviors you've used and how long they controlled your life

   _____

   _____

   _____

2. **Identify the Consequences** – For each addiction, write down the fallout: broken relationships, legal issues, financial losses, health problems, spiritual emptiness.

   _____

   _____

   _____

3. **Unmanageability Questions** – Answer honestly:

   What has addiction cost me physically, emotionally, financially, and spiritually?

   _____

   _____

   _____

   What promises to myself or others have I broken?

   _____

   _____

   _____

How many times have I said, "Never again," but returned anyway?

_____

_____

_____

Who has been hurt by my addiction?

_____

_____

_____

4. **Stop Blaming** – Write down the people or situations you've blamed for your condition. Then cross them out with the words: "I take responsibility for my life."

_____

_____

_____

5. **Admit the Truth** – End with this prayer: _"Lord, I admit I am powerless over my addiction and my life is unmanageable without You. Please show me the way forward."_

Reflection Questions

Looking at your history with drinking or drug use, what were the consequences (legal, relational, financial, health) that followed?

_____

_____

_____

Have you ever promised yourself or others that you would stop, but found you couldn't keep that promise?

_____

_____

_____

Did your addiction ever cause you to lose a job, home, relationship, or opportunity?

_____

_____

_____

How many people were hurt—directly or indirectly—by your addiction?

_____

_____

_____

In what ways have you minimized or denied the impact of your addiction?

_____

_____

_____

What patterns in your life kept repeating even when you wanted to change?

_____

_____

_____

Have you blamed others for the chaos in your life? How has that kept you from taking responsibility?

_____

_____

_____

How did you know today that your life had become unmanageable?

_____

_____

_____

In what ways have I denied or minimized the truth about my addiction?

_____

_____

_____

How has my life become unmanageable (give specific examples)?

_____

_____

_____

What excuses or lies have I told myself to avoid admitting powerlessness?

_____

_____

_____

Who have I hurt by refusing to face the truth?

_____

_____

_____

What do I fear most about surrendering control?

_____

_____

_____

Discussion Questions:

What does the word "powerless" mean to you personally?

_____

_____

_____

_____

What patterns of unmanageability do you see in your own story?

_____

_____

_____

_____

How do denial, minimization, or blame keep us trapped?

_____

_____

_____

_____

Why is honesty with yourself, God, and others so important at this step?

_____

_____

_____

_____

Practical Application

- Begin a daily honesty practice: each morning, write one way you will live in truth today.
- Share one part of your Step 1 inventory with a trusted mentor or peer.
- Memorize John 8:32 (NIV) *"Then you will know the truth, and the truth will set you free."* Repeat it when tempted to minimize.

Choice Point

Recovery is a choice, not a feeling. Step 1 places us at a crossroads:

- Will I keep pretending I'm in control, or will I admit my powerlessness?
- Will I keep blaming others, or will I take responsibility for my life?
- Will I cling to denial, or will I face the truth with courage?

Today, I choose to stop lying to myself. I choose to admit that my life has become unmanageable and that I cannot do this on my own.

Long-Term Reflection – Step 1

In the beginning, admitting I was powerless felt humiliating. Everything in me fought against it, because my whole life I had been told that strength meant control and independence. To say "I am powerless" felt like admitting I was nothing.

But over time, I began to see powerlessness differently. It wasn't humiliation, it was freedom. I didn't have to be God. I didn't have to control people, outcomes, or every detail of my life. That burden wasn't mine to carry.

After a few years in recovery, I noticed that powerlessness wasn't just about drugs and alcohol. It was about my need to control everything—my family, my finances, my reputation, even how others saw me. The more I tried to control it, the more frustrated I became. Step 1 reminded me again and again: control is an illusion, and surrender is the truth.

Now, after decades of sobriety, I can honestly say that Step 1 is not a one-time event but a lifelong practice. Even after 40 years, I still find myself having to surrender daily. But instead of resenting it, I see it as a relief. Step 1 is the reminder that I don't have to run the world, fix everyone, or hold everything together. My job is to admit my limits, and God's job is to show His power in my weakness.

Powerlessness was the most frightening truth at the start of my recovery—but today, it's the foundation of my freedom.

Closing Prayer: *"Lord, I confess that my life has become unmanageable and that I am powerless on my own. I lay down my denial, my excuses, and my blame. I surrender my chaos to You. Take my brokenness and begin to rebuild my life through Your strength. Amen."*

STEP 2

We came to believe that a Power greater than ourselves could restore us to sanity.

Scripture Foundation

"For God has not given us a spirit of fear, but of power and of love and of a sound mind." (2 Timothy 1:7) (KJV)

"Jesus looked at them and said, 'With man this is impossible, but with God all things are possible.'" (Matthew 19:26) (NIV)

"Be still, and know that I am God." (Psalm 46:10) (KJV)

"I will restore to you the years that the locust has eaten." (Joel 2:25) (KJV)

"Do not conform to the pattern of this world, but be transformed by the renewing of your mind." (Romans 12:2) (NIV)

Introduction – The Hope of Sanity Restored

If Step 1 is about facing the truth of our brokenness, Step 2 is about finding hope. Addiction leaves us in insanity—doing the same destructive things over and over, expecting different results. Step 2 invites us to believe that there is a Power greater than ourselves that can restore order to the chaos. For us, that Power is not vague—it is the living God revealed in Jesus Christ.

Step 2 is about faith. Once we admit our powerlessness, the next step is to believe that God can do for us what we cannot do for ourselves. Addiction distorts our thinking, leaving us hopeless and unable to trust. But God promises restoration—not only of sanity, but of a new way of living.

This step is the bridge between despair and transformation. We have admitted we are powerless; now we must come to believe that God is powerful enough to restore what addiction has destroyed. Step 2 is not about perfecting our faith—it is about taking the first steps toward trusting that God can do for us what we cannot do for ourselves.

Belief doesn't mean we have all the answers. It means we are willing to trust God's character, His Word, and His power to heal and transform us. Step 2 reminds us: we don't have to fix ourselves—God is the One who restores.

Teaching & Lesson Content

1. The Insanity of Addiction

Insanity in recovery doesn't mean "crazy" in a medical sense. It means living stuck in destructive cycles, repeating the same mistakes, and expecting a different outcome. Proverbs 26:11 says, *"As a dog returns to its vomit, so fools repeat their folly."* Addiction traps us in that endless loop.

We tell ourselves, "This time will be different," yet we find ourselves right back where we started—broken, ashamed, and defeated. We know the consequences, yet we keep choosing the same path. That is the insanity of addiction.

Addiction convinces us of lies:

- "I can control this."
- "One more time won't hurt."
- "I'm only hurting myself."
- "I can quit whenever I want."

These distortions keep us trapped. Step 2 forces us to see the futility of self-will: we cannot think or willpower our way out of addiction. We need something—Someone—greater than ourselves.

2. The God Who Restores

The word "restore" means to bring back to original condition, to heal what is broken, to repair what has been lost. This is exactly what God promises: *"I will restore to you the years that the locust has eaten"* (Joel 2:25) (KJV).

Step 2 asks us to believe—not in our own strength, not in a vague higher power of our choosing, but in the God who created us, loves us, and has the power to make us whole again. This is the God who raised Jesus from the dead, who heals the brokenhearted, who sets captives free. He is not distant or indifferent. He is actively working to restore what addiction has stolen from us.

God's restoration includes:

- **Mental restoration** – clarity of thought, sound judgment, renewed mind.
- **Emotional restoration** – peace, stability, healing from trauma and shame.
- **Spiritual restoration** – relationship with God, purpose, hope.
- **Relational restoration** – healing broken relationships, building healthy connections.
- **Physical restoration** – health, strength, vitality.

God doesn't just want to make us sober. He wants to make us whole.

3. Faith Is a Choice

Belief doesn't always come with feelings. Some of us start Step 2 unsure if God cares, or even if He exists. We may have been hurt by religion, disappointed by unanswered prayers, or convinced that we are beyond redemption. But Step 2 is less about feelings and more about choice.

Hebrews 11:6 (NIV) says, *"Anyone who comes to Him must believe that He exists and that He rewards those who earnestly seek Him."* Choosing to believe opens the door for God to work, even if we don't feel anything yet.

Faith begins with a simple decision: "I don't have all the answers, but I'm willing to trust that God is greater than me and that He can restore my life."

You don't need perfect faith. You just need to be willing to believe. Even if you're not sure, even if you have doubts, you can pray: *"Lord, I believe; help my unbelief"* (Mark 9:24) (ESV).

4. The Sanity God Provides

Sanity is more than simply being sober. It is clarity of mind, peace of spirit, and the ability to make sound choices. For years, addiction distorted our thinking. We made decisions based on fear, shame, impulse, and desperation. Our minds were clouded, our emotions chaotic, our lives spinning out of control.

Romans 12:2 (NIV) says, *"Do not conform to the pattern of this world, but be transformed by the renewing of your mind."* Step 2 is about trusting God to reorder our thoughts, heal our emotions, and empower us to live differently.

Sanity means:

- We can face life without running to substances or destructive behaviors
- We can experience peace even in difficult circumstances
- Our minds are no longer ruled by addiction, but by the Spirit of God
- We can make sound decisions based on truth, not fear or impulse
- We can think clearly and respond wisely to challenges
- Sanity is not the absence of chaos—it's the presence of God's peace.

5. Hope for the Hopeless

Addiction tells us we are hopeless cases. It whispers that we've gone too far, done too much damage, burned too many bridges. It says that people like us don't get better—we just survive, barely.

But Step 2 insists that no one is too far gone for God to restore. The Gospels are full of broken, hopeless people healed by Jesus—lepers, prostitutes, tax collectors, the demon-possessed. Their restoration reminds us that God delights in lifting up the desperate and setting captives free.

If God could restore them, He can restore us. No matter how deep the pit, God's arm is long enough to reach down and pull us out.

2 Corinthians 5:17 (NIV) says, *"Therefore, if anyone is in Christ, the new creation has come: The old has gone, the new is here!"* This is the hope of Step 2—that God can make us new.

6. Recognizing God's Voice and His Will

Over the years, I've learned that God is not a God of circumstances. Early on, I thought if things looked good on the outside, then it must be God's will. But I discovered that my thoughts and feelings can fool me. Just because something seems good doesn't mean it's from the Lord.

I began to seek God's will in all things—sometimes through His Word, and sometimes through that still, small voice in my spirit. But I had to learn to test what I heard, because my own voice could easily masquerade as His.

Believing that God could restore me to sanity meant more than just hoping He would remove my addiction—it meant trusting Him to renew my mind, my heart, and my entire way of life. That belief became the foundation for my recovery.

How to recognize the difference between your own thoughts and God's leading:

- God's voice aligns with Scripture.
- God's voice brings peace, not confusion (1 Corinthians 14:33 (NIV paraphrased).
- God's voice convicts without condemning (Romans 8:1) (NIV paraphrased).
- God's voice leads to humility, service, and love.
- God's voice is confirmed by wise counsel and circumstances over time.

7. Sanctification and Recovery

Obeying God's Word has become central to my recovery. I now see it as part of the sanctification process. Surrender to Christ saves me, but it doesn't instantly make me holy. Recovery, like sanctification, is a continual process of learning, surrendering, and aligning my will with His.

Step 2 has taught me that faith grows over time. At first, I only believed God could save me from addiction. But over the years, I've come to trust Him with my relationships, my ministry, my future, and even my weaknesses. Sanity is not just the absence of chaos—it's the presence of God's peace.

Sanctification means:

- God is continually working to make us more like Christ.
- We are being transformed from the inside out.
- Growth happens gradually, through daily surrender and obedience.
- We don't become perfect, but we do become more whole.

Recovery and sanctification are intertwined. Both require faith, surrender, and daily dependence on God.

Story Box – My Personal Journey

When I first heard about Step 2, I wasn't sure if it applied to me. I had already admitted my life was unmanageable, but could God really restore me? My life was such a wreck that "sanity" felt out of reach.

The truth is, I had already experienced a taste of God's restoring power in jail. Alone in a cell, I picked up a Bible and began to read. As the days went by, conviction set in. I hit my knees and prayed, desperate for forgiveness and direction. What I experienced in those moments was unlike anything I had ever known—the presence of God, the assurance that I was forgiven, the hope that my life wasn't over.

That was my first step toward believing that God could restore me. Even though I still had doubts, I realized something: I didn't have to know everything about God to start trusting Him. I just had to believe that He was greater than me and that He wanted to make me whole.

In the beginning, I struggled with the idea of faith. I had been let down so many times—by people, by myself, by circumstances. Trusting felt risky. But as I worked Step 2, I began to see small signs of restoration. My thinking became clearer. My emotions started to stabilize. I began to make decisions that didn't destroy me. Slowly, I realized that God was doing for me what I could never do for myself.

Step 2 wasn't about having perfect faith. It was about being willing to believe that restoration was possible. And that willingness opened the door for God to begin His work in my life.

Step 2 Practical Guide – Moving from Despair to Belief

1. List the Insanity

Write down examples of how you've repeated destructive behaviors despite knowing the outcome. Be specific. What patterns kept repeating? What consequences did you ignore?

_____

_____

_____

Examples:

"I kept using even after losing my job, my family, and my health."

"I promised myself I'd quit, but within days I was back at it."

"I knew drinking would lead to a blackout, but I did it anyway."

2. Define Sanity

What would "sanity restored" look like for you? Peace? Clarity? Healthy relationships? Financial stability? The ability to make sound decisions? Write your vision of what a restored life looks like.

_____

_____

_____

Examples:

- "Sanity means I can face stress without running to substances."
- "Sanity means I can think clearly and make wise choices."
- "Sanity means I have peace in my mind and heart."

3. Explore Belief

Be honest: What do you currently believe about God? What doubts or fears do you have? Write them down without judgment. This is where you are starting, and that's okay.

_____

_____

_____

Examples:

- "I'm not sure God cares about me."
- "I've prayed before and nothing changed."
- "I'm afraid I'm too far gone for God to help."

4. Read Scripture

Choose verses about restoration (Joel 2:25; 2 Corinthians 5:17; Romans 12:2; Psalm 23:3). Write what they mean to you personally. How do they speak to your situation?

_____

_____

_____

5. Pray Simply

"God, I don't understand everything, but I believe You are greater than me. Please restore me to sanity. Help my unbelief."

Reflection Questions

What comes to mind when you hear the word "sanity"?

_____

_____

In what ways did your addiction distort your thinking or judgment?

_____

_____

What fears or doubts make it hard for you to trust God?

_____

_____

How have you already seen God working in your life, even in small ways?

_____

_____

What does "restoration" look like for you—mentally, emotionally, spiritually?

_____

_____

What does it mean to trust in a Power greater than yourself?

_____

_____

Where do I see insanity in my life—repeating destructive cycles and expecting different results?

_____

_____

Do I truly believe God has the power to restore me? Why or why not?

_____

_____

What small step of faith can I take today to grow in belief?

_____

_____

Have I seen any evidence—no matter how small—that God is already working in my life?

_____

_____

What would change in my life if I fully believed God could restore me?

_____

_____

How do I recognize the difference between my own thoughts and God's leading?

_____

_____

In what ways has the process of sanctification shown up in my recovery journey?

_____

_____

Discussion Questions

What lies or distortions did your addiction convince you to believe?

_____

_____

How do you know today that God can restore your mind and life?

_____

_____

What is one area where you still struggle to trust God fully?

_____

_____

How can you begin to strengthen your faith in Him daily?

_____

_____

What does "insanity" mean in the context of addiction and recovery?

_____

_____

Why is it important to believe in a Power greater than ourselves?

_____

_____

How does faith differ from feelings?

_____

_____

Can we believe even when we don't feel it?

_____

_____

What does it mean that God "restores" us?

_____

_____

What areas of your life need restoration?

_____

_____

How can we grow in belief when doubt feels overwhelming?

_____

_____

Practical Application

- Begin each morning by asking God for clarity and peace of mind.
- *Identify* one way each day that you see God working to restore order in your life—even small things count.
- Share your Step 2 prayer with a mentor or peer for accountability and encouragement.
- Memorize 2 Timothy 1:7 (KJV) *"For God has not given us a spirit of fear, but of power and of love and of a sound mind."*
- Commit to 10 minutes of daily prayer this week, asking God to increase your faith.
- Choose one Scripture each day to meditate on and carry with you.

Choice Point – Step 2 Step 2 places us at a choice:

- Will I keep trying to fix myself, or will I trust a Power greater than me?
- Will I live in despair, or will I believe in the God who restores?
- Will I choose doubt, or will I take a step of faith?

Today, I choose to believe that God can restore me to sanity. I may not have perfect faith, but I am willing to trust Him one day at a time.

Long-Term Reflection – Step 2

At first, believing God could restore me felt impossible. My life was so broken that the idea of sanity seemed like a fantasy. But over the years, I've learned that belief is not about having it all figured out—it's about choosing to trust Him, one day at a time.

In the early years, that meant simply praying when I didn't feel like it, or opening my Bible when my mind told me it wouldn't help. Slowly, I saw God working: giving me peace in situations where I used to panic, helping me repair relationships I thought were destroyed, teaching me how to make decisions without destroying myself.

Now, decades later, I can say with certainty: God restores. He restored my mind, my hope, and my ability to live in freedom. I am not the same man I was when I began this journey. The insanity that once ruled my life has been replaced with clarity, purpose, and peace.

Step 2 wasn't just about believing once—it's about continuing to believe every day that God is able to do what I cannot. Even after 40 years of sobriety, I still return to this step. When life feels overwhelming, when old patterns try to resurface, when doubt creeps in, I remind myself: God has restored me before, and He will continue to restore me. My job is simply to believe and to keep showing up.

The hope I found in Step 2 has carried me through every challenge, every setback, every moment of weakness. And it will carry you, too.

Closing Prayer

"Lord, I come to You with doubts and fears, but I choose to believe that You are greater than my addiction and my brokenness. I ask You to restore my mind, *Amen.*"

STEP 3

We made a decision to turn our will and our lives over to the care of God.

Scripture Foundation

"Trust in the Lord with all your heart and lean not on your own understanding; in all your ways submit to him, and he will make your paths straight." (Proverbs 3:5–6) (NIV)

"I have been crucified with Christ and I no longer live, but Christ lives in me. The life I now live in the body, I live by faith in the Son of God, who loved me and gave himself for me." (Galatians 2:20) (NIV)

"If anyone would come after me, let him deny himself and take up his cross daily and follow me." (Luke 9:23) (ESV)

Introduction – The Turning Point

Step 3 is the crossroads of recovery. Step 1 showed us the truth: we are powerless. Step 2 gave us hope: God can restore us. Now Step 3 calls for a decision. Will I keep following my will, which has led me to destruction, or will I surrender to God's will, trusting Him to lead me into life?

This is the step of repentance—turning away from a life of self-will and turning toward God. It is also an act of faith. We don't know everything about what the future will hold, but we trust that God's care is better than our control.

Step 3 is about surrender. It is not simply believing in God's power (Step 2) but entrusting our whole lives into His care. This decision requires humility, faith, and willingness. Turning our will over means giving up the illusion of control—laying down the plans, excuses, and self-centeredness that keep us trapped. Turning our lives over means trusting that God not only saves us, but also leads us into a new way of living.

Step 3 is both a moment of decision and a daily practice. It is saying: "Not my will, but Yours be done."

Teaching & Lesson Content

1. The Problem of Self-Will

Our lives fell apart because we insisted on running them our own way. We chased desires, pleasures, and control, but ended up with chaos. The Bible calls this missing the mark—sin. Romans 3:23 (NIV) says, *"For all have sinned and fall short of the glory of God."*

We missed the mark not only with drugs or alcohol but in relationships, finances, priorities, and values. We thought we knew what was best for us. We made plans, set goals, and pursued what we wanted—but our way led to destruction. Every attempt to control our lives on our own terms only deepened the chaos.

Step 3 asks us to admit that our will has failed us. It's not just that we made a few bad choices—it's that the entire direction of our lives was wrong. Our self-will was the problem, and no amount of effort could fix it. We need a new direction, and that direction can only come from God.

2. The Choice to Surrender

Step 3 is about more than believing in God—it's about choosing to trust Him with our lives. Proverbs 3:5–6 (NIV) says, *"Trust in the Lord with all your heart and lean not on your own understanding; in all your ways submit to him, and he will make your paths straight."*

Surrender is not passive; it is an active choice to stop relying on our broken will and to entrust ourselves to God's care. It means letting go of the need to control outcomes, manipulate circumstances, or force our way through life. It means saying, "God, I don't know what's best for me, but You do. I'm giving You control."

This is terrifying for many of us. We've spent our whole lives trying to be in charge, trying to protect ourselves, trying to make things work. But Step 3 asks us to lay all of that down and trust that God's plan is better than ours.

3. Repentance: Turning From and Turning To

The word "repent" simply means to turn around, to change direction. In Step 3, we turn away from self-destruction and toward God's way of living. This doesn't mean we suddenly become perfect, but it does mean we commit to a new path.

Acts 3:19 (NIV) says, *"Repent, then, and turn to God, so that your sins may be wiped out, that times of refreshing may come from the Lord."* When we surrender, God not only forgives us but begins to refresh and rebuild us. Repentance is not about shame or self-condemnation, it's about hope. It's about choosing a new direction and trusting God to lead us there.

Step 3 is the moment we stop running from God and start running toward Him. We stop trying to save ourselves and let Him save us. We stop insisting on our way and start following His.

4. The Exchange of Values

Turning our lives over to God also means exchanging our values for His. Our old values—selfishness, pride, lust, envy, resentment—have only kept us trapped. God's values—love, humility, truth, faithfulness—are the foundation of a new life.

In Step 4, we will examine these values more deeply, but Step 3 sets the stage by committing us to live not by our will, but by His. We begin to ask ourselves: "What does God value? How does He want me to live? What kind of person does He want me to become?" These questions guide us as we learn to surrender daily.

5. The Act of Faith

Step 3 is an act of faith. We don't surrender because we have it all figured out. We surrender because we trust that God knows better than we do. Hebrews 11:1 (NIV) says, *"Now faith is confidence in what we hope for and assurance about what we do not see."*

Faith says, "God, I don't know where this path will lead, but I trust You to guide me." It means taking a step forward even when we can't see the outcome. It means believing that God's care is real, even when we don't feel it yet.

Surrender is not a one-time event. It is a daily practice. Every morning, we wake up and choose again: "Today, I will follow God's will, not my own." Some days that choice feels easy. Other days it feels impossible. But each time we choose to surrender, we grow stronger in faith.

Story Box – My Personal Journey

I was put in segregation in jail after I threatened to kill someone while coming off drugs. At first, I didn't even realize where I was. But I had a Bible in my cell, so I began to read it—starting in the New Testament.

After about a week, conviction fell heavily on me. I got down on my knees and began to pray. I cried out to Jesus Christ for forgiveness and answers to my life. Suddenly, His presence overwhelmed me. I fell to the floor, sobbing uncontrollably. For three days, my whole life flashed before me.

The Lord spoke to me: "You are forgiven and you now belong to me." For the first time, I knew I was completely loved and redeemed. Then He spoke again: "You are going to be released from jail and not even have a felony." At the time, that seemed impossible—but 60 days later, I was released with no felony, just treatment.

Even the jailers noticed the change. They said, "You act like you like it here and are happy all the time." They didn't know that I was happy—because I had been forgiven. I belonged to Jesus. That was the day I truly turned my will and life over to Him.

When I came to Step 3, I was exhausted. I had tried to control every area of my life—relationships, money, reputation—and every attempt only led me deeper into chaos. I knew my way wasn't working.

The hardest part was admitting that my way wasn't just broken—it was destructive. I had to face the truth: my will had missed the mark. The more I tried to hold on, the worse things got. Step 3 asked me to do something I had avoided my whole life: surrender.

When I finally turned my will and my life over to God, something changed. I didn't suddenly become perfect, but I felt the weight lift. I knew I didn't have to run the world anymore. I didn't have to fix everything. I could trust God to guide me, one day at a time.

Looking back, I realize surrender is not just a one-time event in a jail cell. God delivered me in that moment, but He has kept teaching me to surrender daily ever since. His timing is not mine—He promised release, but I had to wait 60 days. He promised forgiveness, but sanctification has been a lifelong process.

Over the years, I've learned that surrender is about giving God control over every area—addictions, yes, but also my relationships, my ministry, my witness. His voice is steady, even when life is not. The surrender I began that day is still shaping my life today.

Worksheet: Learning to Surrender

Step 3 Practical Guide – Learning to Surrender

Write Down Your Will – List the areas of life you've tried to control (relationships, finances, work, emotions, reputation, future plans).

_____

_____

_____

Identify the Results – For each area, describe how your will has missed the mark. What has been the outcome of trying to control these areas on your own?

_____

_____

_____

Name God's Way – Write down what God's will might look like in that same area (peace instead of chaos, truth instead of lies, love instead of selfishness, trust instead of fear).

_____

_____

_____

Pray a Surrender Prayer – Example: _"God, I admit my way has failed me. I turn my will and my life over to You. Lead me in Your ways, and help me trust You."_

_____

_____

_____

Take One Step – Choose one area of your life and make a practical decision that reflects God's will instead of your own. What is one action you can take today that demonstrates surrender?

_____

_____

_____

Reflection Questions

What areas of your life do you still try to control?

_____

_____

_____

Why is it hard to surrender your will to God?

_____

_____

_____

What does it mean for you to trust God with your future?

_____

_____

_____

How can you practice surrender in small, daily choices?

_____

_____

_____

Who or what have you placed your trust in before, and how did that turn out?

_____

_____

_____

What would it look like to truly give God your entire life today?

_____

_____

_____

Where has my will missed the mark?

_____

_____

_____

What fears keep me from fully surrendering to God?

_____

_____

_____

What values do I need to let go of to live according to God's will?

_____

_____

_____

In what area of my life do I need to trust God today?

_____

_____

_____

What does it mean for me personally to "turn my life over to God's care"?

_____

_____

_____

Discussion Questions

What does surrender mean to you personally?

_____

_____

_____

Why is Step 3 more than just believing in God—why is it about turning everything over to Him?

_____

_____

_____

What fears do you have about giving God total control?

_____

_____

_____

What would change in your life if you truly entrusted it all to Him today?

_____

_____

_____

How is repentance different from just feeling sorry for our mistakes?

_____

_____

_____

What does it mean to exchange our values for God's values?

_____

_____

_____

Practical Application

- Each morning, pray a simple prayer of surrender: *"God, I give You my will and my life today. Guide my steps."*
- Share with a mentor or sponsor one specific area where you are struggling to let go of control.
- Begin to practice aligning your daily decisions with God's values, not your desires.
- Memorize Proverbs 3:5–6 and repeat it when you feel the urge to take back control.

Choice Point

Step 3 places us at a decision point:

- Will I continue following my own will, knowing it leads to destruction?
- Or will I surrender my will and my life to God, trusting Him to lead me into freedom?
- Will I keep trying to control outcomes, or will I trust God's timing and His plan?

Today, I choose to surrender. I choose to turn my will and my life over to God's care. I may not understand everything, but I trust that His way is better than mine.

Long-Term Reflection – Step 3

In the beginning, surrender felt terrifying. I thought turning my life over to God meant losing control completely. What I've learned over the years is that surrender is not loss—it's freedom.

I've discovered that my will, left unchecked, always pulls me back toward selfishness and destruction. But when I surrender, God gives me strength to live differently. Over time, I've learned that surrender isn't just for the "big" issues—it's for everyday choices: how I treat people, how I handle money, how I respond when I'm hurt.

What does surrender mean to me today compared to when I first began recovery? It means peace. It means knowing that I don't have to carry the weight of the world on my shoulders. It means trusting that God's timing is different from mine—and that His timing is always right.

Looking back after decades, I see that Step 3 was the turning point of my recovery. It was the moment I decided that my way was not enough and that God's way was the only way. That decision didn't just keep me sober—it gave me a new life.

Even now, after 40 years, I still practice Step 3 daily. Every morning, I wake up and choose to surrender again. Some days it's easy. Other days, I have to fight the urge to take back control. But each time I surrender, I experience the freedom that comes from trusting God instead of myself.

Step 3 is not a one-time decision—it's a lifelong practice. And it's the foundation of everything that follows.

Closing Prayer

"Lord, today I turn my will and my life over to You. Take my fears, my plans, and my self-centered ways, and replace them with Your peace and direction. Help me to walk in daily surrender, trusting that Your will is better than mine. I don't have all the answers, but I trust that You do. Lead me, guide me, and give me the courage to follow You one day at a time. Amen."

STEP 4

We made a searching and fearless moral inventory of ourselves.

Scripture Foundation

"Search me, O God, and know my heart; test me and know my anxious thoughts. See if there is any offensive way in me and lead me in the way everlasting." (Psalm 139:23–24) (NIV)

"Therefore confess your sins to each other and pray for each other so that you may be healed." (James 5:16) (NIV)

"Then you will know the truth, and the truth will set you free." (John 8:32) (NIV)

Introduction – The Courage to Face the Truth

Step 4 is where we stop running from ourselves. Addiction taught us to hide, deny, and cover up. Step 4 calls us to be fearless—to shine God's light into every corner of our hearts and uncover the truth about our character.

This is not about condemnation. It is about discovery. We write down our resentments, fears, relationships, and patterns, so we can see clearly where sin and brokenness have shaped our lives. Only then can God begin to heal and restore.

Step 4 is one of the hardest steps in recovery, but also one of the most freeing. It requires us to stop hiding, stop pretending, and begin uncovering the truth about who we are. The purpose of a moral inventory is not to shame us but to free us. We put on paper the hurts, habits, and hang-ups that have shaped our lives. By shining light into the darkness, we strip shame of its power and give God permission to heal what has been broken.

Honesty is the foundation of Step 4. Many of us fear that if others really knew us, they would reject us— or that if we confessed everything to God, He would stop loving us. But the truth is that God already knows and loves us anyway. The inventory is for our healing, not His information.

Step 4 is where honesty becomes healing. You're not writing an inventory to beat yourself up; you're inviting God to bring truth into the places that hurt so He can restore you. Many destructive patterns begin at the root of pain—wounds that were spiritual, emotional, mental, or physical. Whether that hurt was actual or perceived, your perception shaped your beliefs, your beliefs shaped your coping, and your coping shaped your choices. Step 4 helps you trace that path so you can finally break the cycle.

Teaching & Lesson Content

1. Truth Heals What Hiding Cannot

Secrets keep us sick. Shame grows in the dark. Bringing our story into the light with God is not condemnation—it's care. Jesus meets people in truth and offers mercy and transformation (John 8:11).

We spend years hiding from ourselves, from others, and from God. We build walls of denial, minimization, and blame to protect ourselves from facing the truth. But those walls don't protect us—they imprison us. Step 4 invites us to tear down the walls and let God's light shine into every hidden place.

2. Why We Write It Down

The inventory must be written to be honest and specific. When we only think about our issues, we can rationalize, minimize, or avoid them. But when we put pen to paper, we are forced to be concrete and truthful. Writing makes it real. It helps us see patterns we've been blind to and uncover roots we didn't know existed.

3. Fearless Honesty

Hiding protects our pride, but honesty brings healing. Step 4 calls us to be "fearless"—not because we're naturally brave, but because we trust that God's grace is greater than our sin. We don't have to be afraid of what we'll find when we look inside, because God already knows and He's not going anywhere.

Romans 8:1 (NIV) reminds us: *"Therefore, there is now no condemnation for those who are in Christ Jesus."* God convicts to heal; the enemy condemns to paralyze. Step 4 is about conviction, not condemnation.

4. The Root System of Addiction

Understanding how addiction develops helps us see why Step 4 is so important. Here's a simple map of how hurt becomes habit:

→**HURT** (wounds, neglect, abandonment, abuse, betrayal)

→**BELIEFS FORMED** ("I'm not safe," "I'm unlovable," "It's on me to survive")

→**COPING** ("numb out," "perform," "control," "please," "explode," "hide")

→**BEHAVIORS** (use, lie, isolate, rage, sexual acting out, overspend, etc.)

→**CONSEQUENCES** (damage, guilt)

→**SHAME** ("I am the problem")

→ **MORE HURT** → the cycle repeats.

Step 4 helps you name the hurt, challenge the lies, and exchange broken coping for God's way. It breaks the cycle by bringing truth into every part of the pattern.

5. Trauma and Responsibility—Holding Both with Wisdom

- **If you were abused or mistreated:** that is not your fault. We name it plainly. In your inventory, you'll list "Harms Received" to honor the truth and seek care.
- **Where you've harmed others:** we tell the truth there, too. We own our side—without excusing the harm done to us (Galatians 6:5).
- **Guilt vs. shame:** guilt says, "I did wrong." Shame says, "I am wrong." God convicts to heal; the enemy condemns to paralyze (Romans 8:1).

6. What a Moral Inventory Is—and Isn't

It is:

- A structured look at resentments, fears, harms, patterns, and values, so you can see causes and conditions with God's help.
- An honest assessment of where you've missed the mark and where you've been wounded.
- A tool for clarity, confession, and change.

It is not:

- A rant or a court case against others.
- A journal of self-hatred or self-condemnation.
- An excuse to blame others for your choices.

The goal is clarity → confession → change.

7. God's Values vs. My Survival Values

Step 3 said, "I'm turning from my will to God's will." Step 4 shows where my values (self-protection, control, image, instant relief) have missed the mark and invites God's values (truth, humility, love, purity, service, patience) to take root.

Our old values kept us trapped. God's values set us free. Step 4 helps us identify which values we've been living by and which ones need to be exchanged for God's truth.

8. Your Thinking Lens Matters (Perception & Distortions)

Common distortions include:

- **All-or-nothing thinking:** "I always fail."
- **Mind-reading:** "They hate me."
- **Catastrophizing:** "This will ruin everything."

Step 4 notes where these lenses appear so Scripture and truth can correct them. Romans 12:2 (NIV) says, *"Do not conform to the pattern of this world, but be transformed by the renewing of your mind."*

9. Patterns and Defects

Step 4 uncovers the deeper character defects behind our actions. It's not just about what we did—it's about why we did it. What patterns keep repeating? What defects (selfishness, dishonesty, fear, pride, lust, greed, envy, anger) drive our behavior?

Identifying these patterns is the first step toward letting God remove them.

10. God's Light

This is not about self-condemnation, but allowing God to reveal the truth. Psalm 139:23–24 (NIV) is our prayer: *"Search me, O God, and know my heart; test me and know my anxious thoughts. See if there is any offensive way in me, and lead me in the way everlasting."*

We invite God into the process. We ask Him to show us what we need to see, and we trust that His purpose is healing, not punishment.

11. Safety and Support: Pace With Wisdom

This work can stir memories. You're not weak if you need help. Use grounding techniques (breath, feet on floor, orient to room), take breaks, and—when needed—process with a Peer Recovery Support Specialist or a Licensed Therapist.

Heart Renewed provides whole-person support: PRSS, case management, and licensed counseling are available. You don't have to do this alone.

Story Box – My Personal Journey

When I first started writing out my moral inventory, I wasn't completely honest. I thought, "If people really knew who I was, they would want nothing to do with me." Even worse, part of me believed that if I didn't confess everything to God, maybe He wouldn't know how bad I really was—and He would still love me.

I was playing mind games with myself. I thought I could control the outcome by hiding pieces of the truth. But over time, I learned that the very things I tried to hide were the things keeping me in chains.

When I sat down to write my first inventory, I froze. I thought, "If you really knew me, you'd walk away." I even tried to hide parts from God—as if He didn't already know. What I discovered was that fear and shame were guarding old hurts I had never named. As I wrote, I didn't just see my "bad choices"; I saw the pain that taught me to grab control and numb out.

I felt ashamed and afraid. I thought, "If you really knew who I was, you wouldn't even talk to me anymore." But as I kept writing, I realized God already knew everything—and He still loved me. Writing my inventory helped me uncover resentments, fears, and shame that I had buried for years. It wasn't easy, but it was the first time I could truly see myself clearly.

When I finally shared my full inventory with another person and with God, I began to experience freedom. Telling the truth—first to God, then to a trusted person—didn't crush me; it freed me. It was the beginning of real change. It wasn't easy, but it was worth it. Step 4 taught me that secrecy is bondage, but honesty is the pathway to healing.

Before moving into Step 4 and writing out our moral inventory we need to learn what morals are and understand what moral code we have been operating from and then learn what moral code we want to live by. The following study will help you to understand who you really are:

"Practice Makes Character"

Values don't grow in theory — they grow through practice. When you commit to a 30-Day Challenge, you're telling God, *I'm ready to live what I believe.* Each small choice shapes the person you're becoming.

Don't get discouraged if you stumble. Every fall is another lesson in humility and grace. God doesn't grade perfection; He blesses progress.

Reflection Verse: "Let us not become weary in doing good, for at the proper time we will reap a harvest if we do not give up." — *Galatians 6:9 (NIV)*

Think About: What value do I want to become automatic in my life? What can I do daily to build that muscle?

"Values in Real Life"

It's easy to say what we believe — harder to live it when things get tough. The scenarios that follow help you practice your values when life squeezes you.

Each situation is a mirror showing who you were and who you're becoming. Don't rush through them — imagine yourself there. Ask, *What would Christ do in this moment?* Then, let that answer guide you.

Reflection Verse: "Do not merely listen to the word, and so deceive yourselves. Do what it says." — *James 1:22 (NIV)*

Think About: How can I respond with values instead of reactions? What would the "new me" do differently?

MORAL VALUES DISCOVERY & ASSESSMENT

PART A: ADDICTION REALITY CHECK

1. During my active addiction, what did I really value most? (Be brutally honest)

- Getting high/drunk

- Avoiding consequences

- Getting what I wanted in the moment

- Other: _____

2. List 3 ways addiction destroyed my moral compass:

1. _____

2. _____

3. _____

3. What values did I abandon or never develop?

Honesty   **Responsibility**   **Respect**   **Integrity**   **Compassion**

Humility   **Gratitude**   **Other:** _____

PART B: VALUES DISCOVERY

Circle the values that are most important to you NOW:

Core Values:

- Honesty
- Responsibility
- Respect
- Integrity
- Compassion
- Humility
- Gratitude
- Faith
- Family
- Friendship
- Hard Work
- Service
- Growth
- Peace
- Joy

A weekly evaluation tool has been included to see how well you are practicing each value. Prayerfully, as you progress over time each one of these moral values will gain in their importance to you as your moral compass evolves into who you were created to be.

These values should all be studied completely before you move onto your 4th Step Inventory.

CORE VALUES — DEFINITIONS, EXAMPLES & REFLECTIONS

1. Honesty

Definition: Telling the truth to yourself, to God, and to others — even when it's uncomfortable.
Examples:

- Admitting it when you're struggling instead of hiding it.
- Returning something that isn't yours.
- Being truthful on your daily check-in.
  Reflection: "The truth sets us free, but lies keep us chained." — *John 8:32 paraphrased*

Why This Matters:
Honesty is the foundation of all healing. In addiction, deceit becomes a survival tool — we hide, deny, and justify. But recovery begins when we stop lying to ourselves and let the truth in. Every time we tell the truth, we weaken the grip of shame and strengthen our relationship with God and others.

How to Practice This Daily:
• Admit mistakes instead of making excuses.
• Tell your mentor or peer how you really feel.
• Be truthful on your daily check-in or inventory.
• Return lost or borrowed items promptly.
• Speak the truth in love — not anger.

Reflection Questions:

What is one truth about myself I've been avoiding?

_____

_____

How does being honest make me feel — free or fearful?

_____

_____

What can I do this week to build a habit of truth-telling?

_____

_____

Bible Connection:
Jesus called Himself *"the Truth."* When we walk in honesty, we walk in His light and freedom.
"Then you will know the truth, and the truth will set you free." — *John 8:32(NIV)*

Rate yourself 1–5 daily (1 = Never, 2 = Rarely, 3 = Sometimes, 4 = Often, 5 = Always)

Question	Mon	Tue	Wed	Thu	Fri	Sat	Sun
I told the truth even when it was hard.							
I admitted when I didn't know something.							
I was honest about my feelings or struggles.							
Weekly Average:							

Why is honesty an important moral value to me?

_____

_____

2. Responsibility

Definition: Owning your actions, choices, and duties instead of blaming others.
Examples:

- Showing up on time for work or group.
- Making your bed without being told.
- Apologizing when you've hurt someone.
  Reflection: "Each one should carry their own load." — *Galatians 6:5*

Why This Matters:
Freedom grows when we stop blaming others and start owning our lives. Responsibility rebuilds the character that addiction tore down. It transforms "I have to" into "I get to" — a mindset of maturity, accountability, and gratitude for the opportunity to grow.

How to Practice This Daily:
• Follow through on chores and commitments.
• Be on time for groups, work, and meetings.
• Admit when you're wrong without excuses.
• Keep your personal area and schedule organized.
• Take initiative without being told.

Reflection Questions:

Where have I blamed others for my own choices?

_____

_____

What responsibilities can I take more seriously this week?

_____

_____

How does responsibility show spiritual maturity?

_____

_____

Bible Connection:
God entrusts us with responsibilities as a sign of His trust. Taking ownership honors Him and builds strength.
"Each one should carry their own load." — *Galatians 6:5 (NIV)*

Rate yourself 1–5 daily (1 = Never, 2 = Rarely, 3 = Sometimes, 4 = Often, 5 = Always)

Question	Mon	Tue	Wed	Thu	Fri	Sat	Sun
I completed tasks without reminders.							
I owned my mistakes instead of making excuses.							
I showed up on time and prepared for my responsibilities.							
Weekly Average:							

Why is responsibility an important moral value to me?

_____

3. Respect

Definition: Treating people, property, and yourself with honor and care.
Examples:

- Listening when someone else is speaking.
- Keeping shared spaces clean.
- Speaking kindly to others, even when frustrated.
  Reflection: "Show proper respect to everyone." — *1 Peter 2:17 (NIV)*

Why This Matters:
Disrespect is one of the first casualties of addiction — it leads to broken trust, conflict, and chaos. Learning respect helps restore order and peace. When you respect yourself and others, you show God that you value His creation and His people.

How to Practice This Daily:
• Listen without interrupting.
• Speak kindly even when you disagree.
• Clean up after yourself in shared spaces.
• Honor staff, mentors, and peers alike.
• Respect your own body by staying healthy and sober.

Reflection Questions:

How does showing respect change the atmosphere around me?

_____

_____

Who in my life deserves more respect from me right now?

_____

_____

How can I show respect to myself today?

_____

_____

Bible Connection:
Respect begins with recognizing that every person is made in God's image — including you.
"Show proper respect to everyone." — 1 Peter 2:17 (NIV)

Rate yourself 1–5 daily (1 = Never, 2 = Rarely, 3 = Sometimes, 4 = Often, 5 = Always)

Question	Mon	Tue	Wed	Thu	Fri	Sat	Sun
I listened when others were speaking.							
I treated staff and residents with kindness and patience.							
I took care of shared spaces and property.							
Weekly Average:							

Why is respect moral value important to me?

---

4. Integrity

Definition: Doing the right thing even when no one is watching.
Examples:

- Turning in found money instead of keeping it.
- Being honest about time cards or chores done.
- Staying faithful to your commitments.
  Reflection: "Whoever walks in integrity walks securely." — *Proverbs 10:9 (NIV)*

Why This Matters:
Integrity is the inner strength to make right choices for the right reasons. It's the moral backbone of recovery — the difference between living a lie and walking in truth. Without integrity, change doesn't last. With it, character grows solid and trustworthy.

How to Practice This Daily:
• Do your work well even when no one checks.
• Keep promises and commitments.
• Avoid shortcuts that compromise values.
• Confess quickly when you've done wrong.
• Let your actions match your words.

Reflection Questions:

When did I do the right thing even though it cost me?

_____

_____

What small area of my life needs more integrity?

_____

_____

How does integrity bring peace of mind?

_____

_____

Bible Connection:
God values truth in the inward parts. Integrity aligns your heart with His.
"Whoever walks in integrity walks securely." — Proverbs 10:9 (NIV)

Rate yourself 1–5 daily (1 = Never, 2 = Rarely, 3 = Sometimes, 4 = Often, 5 = Always)

Question	Mon	Tue	Wed	Thu	Fri	Sat	Sun
I did what was right when no one was watching.							
My actions matched my words.							
I kept my commitments and promises.							
Weekly Average:							

Why is integrity an important moral value to me?

_____

5. Compassion

Definition: Feeling for others and taking action to help them.
Examples:

- Checking on a roommate who seems down.
- Helping with chores when someone is sick.
- Forgiving someone who wronged you.
  Reflection: "Be kind and compassionate to one another." — *Ephesians 4:32(NIV)*

Why This Matters:
Compassion turns pain into purpose. In recovery, we remember what brokenness feels like, so we can reach others with empathy. Compassion softens a hardened heart and restores love to those who once lived in selfishness or isolation.

How to Practice This Daily:
• Offer to help someone struggling.
• Listen without judgment.
• Pray for someone in pain.
• Forgive quickly and let go of resentment.
• Speak encouragement, not criticism.

Reflection Questions:

How can I show compassion to someone I find difficult to love?

_____

_____

When has someone's compassion helped me grow?

_____

_____

What does real compassion look like in action?

_____

_____

Bible Connection:
Jesus showed compassion to the hurting, the outcast, and the lost. When we care for others, we reflect His heart.
"Be kind and compassionate to one another." — Ephesians 4:32(NIV)

Rate yourself 1–5 daily (1 = Never, 2 = Rarely, 3 = Sometimes, 4 = Often, 5 = Always)

Compassion

Question	Mon	Tue	Wed	Thu	Fri	Sat	Sun
I showed care for someone who was struggling.							
I offered help without expecting anything in return.							
I forgave someone who wronged me today.							
Weekly Average:							

Why is compassion an important moral value to me?

---

6. Humility

Definition: Knowing that you still have room to grow — choosing teachability over pride.
Examples:

- Accepting correction without attitude.
- Asking for help when you need it.
- Giving God credit for your progress.
  Reflection: "God opposes the proud but gives grace to the humble." — *James 4:6 (ESV)*

Why This Matters:
Pride isolates; humility connects. When we admit our need for God and others, true change begins. Humility helps us learn, listen, and stay grateful instead of entitled. It keeps recovery alive and relationships healthy.

How to Practice This Daily:
• Accept correction without arguing.
• Ask for help when you need it.
• Give credit to others for their efforts.
• Serve quietly without needing recognition.
• Remember that every good thing comes from God.

Reflection Questions:

What does humility look like for me today?

_____

_____

When has pride caused me to stumble?

_____

_____

How can humility strengthen my relationships?

_____

_____

Bible Connection:
Jesus humbled Himself to serve others — even washing the disciples' feet. That's the model of true greatness.
"God opposes the proud but gives grace to the humble." — James 4:6 (ESV)

Rate yourself 1–5 daily (1 = Never, 2 = Rarely, 3 = Sometimes, 4 = Often, 5 = Always)

Question	Mon	Tue	Wed	Thu	Fri	Sat	Sun
I accepted correction without arguing.							
I asked for help when I needed it.							
I gave credit to others and to God for my progress.							
Weekly Average:							

Why is humility an important moral value to me?

_____

7. Gratitude

Definition: Choosing to see what's good and thank God for it daily.
Examples:

- Writing one thing you're thankful for each night.
- Saying thank you to staff or peers.
- Noticing how far you've come instead of complaining.
  Reflection: "In everything give thanks." — *1 Thessalonians 5:18 (KJV)*

Why This Matters:
Gratitude changes everything. It turns what we have into enough and transforms recovery from obligation into joy. A thankful heart helps us stay humble and focused on God's faithfulness instead of what we lack.

How to Practice This Daily:
• Write three things you're grateful for each morning.
• Verbally thank staff, mentors, and peers.
• Replace complaints with praise.
• Thank God before meals and meetings.
• Look for blessings in small moments.

Reflection Questions:

What am I grateful for right now, even if life feels hard?

_____

_____

How does gratitude change my mood and mindset?

_____

_____

Who do I need to thank today?

_____

_____

Bible Connection:
A grateful heart invites God's presence and peace.
"In everything give thanks." — 1 Thessalonians 5:18 (KJV)

Rate yourself 1–5 daily (1 = Never, 2 = Rarely, 3 = Sometimes, 4 = Often, 5 = Always)

Question	Mon	Tue	Wed	Thu	Fri	Sat	Sun
I thanked God for today's blessings.							
I expressed thanks to others for their help.							
I focused on what I have rather than what I lack.							
Weekly Average:							

Why is gratitude an important moral value to me?

---

8. Faith

Definition: Trusting God's plan, even when you can't see the outcome.
Examples:

- Praying instead of worrying.
- Believing recovery is possible for you.
- Reading God's Word daily to build strength.
  Reflection: "We walk by faith, not by sight." — *2 Corinthians 5:7 (KJV)*

Why This Matters:
Faith gives us strength when logic and feelings fail. It reminds us that we're not in control — and that's good news. Faith grows through obedience and trust, helping us stay steady when life gets uncertain.

How to Practice This Daily:
• Start your day with prayer or scripture.
• Speak faith over your situation, not fear.
• Trust God's timing instead of forcing results.
• Journal answered prayers.
• Surround yourself with people of faith.

Reflection Questions:

What am I trusting God for right now?

_____

_____

How has faith helped me stay steady in recovery?

_____

_____

What does it mean to "walk by faith, not sight"?

_____

_____

Bible Connection:
Faith isn't about seeing the whole path — just taking the next right step with God.
"We walk by faith, not by sight." — 2 Corinthians 5:7 (KJV)

Rate yourself 1–5 daily (1 = Never, 2 = Rarely, 3 = Sometimes, 4 = Often, 5 = Always)

Question	Mon	Tue	Wed	Thu	Fri	Sat	Sun
I trusted God when I couldn't see the outcome.							
I prayed before making decisions.							
I chose faith over fear in difficult moments.							
Weekly Average:							

Why is Faith important to me as a moral value?

_____

9. Family

Definition: Valuing relationships built on love, loyalty, and forgiveness.
Examples:

- Making amends to your loved ones.
- Setting boundaries that protect peace.
- Becoming a positive role model to children or siblings.
  Reflection: "As for me and my house, we will serve the Lord." — *Joshua 24:15 (KJV)*

Why This Matters:
Addiction tears families apart — but God specializes in restoration. Family isn't just blood; it's the people God gives us to love and grow with. When we rebuild trust and learn to forgive, we create a new foundation of peace and support for ourselves and those we love.

How to Practice This Daily:
• Reach out to family with humility and honesty.
• Apologize when you've caused pain.
• Set healthy boundaries that promote peace.
• Participate in family activities or phone calls with respect.
• Pray for your family daily.

Reflection Questions:

What relationships in my family need healing?

_____

_____

How can I show love even if trust isn't fully restored?

_____

_____

How does forgiveness create a new kind of family strength?

_____

_____

Bible Connection:
God places the lonely in families and calls us to love one another deeply.
"As for me and my house, we will serve the Lord." — Joshua 24:15 (KJV)

Rate yourself 1–5 daily (1 = Never, 2 = Rarely, 3 = Sometimes, 4 = Often, 5 = Always)

Question	Mon	Tue	Wed	Thu	Fri	Sat	Sun
I communicated with my family respectfully.							
I worked to rebuild trust with loved ones.							
I prayed for my family and their healing.							
Weekly Average:							

Why is Family important to me as a moral value?

---

10. Friendship

Definition: Building relationships based on trust, respect, and shared growth.
Examples:

- Being a friend who listens, not just talks.
- Encouraging someone who's having a hard day.
- Keeping confidence when someone shares personally.
  Reflection: "A friend loves at all times." — *Proverbs 17:17 (NIV)*

Why This Matters:
Real friendship isn't about using people — it's about walking together toward growth and accountability. In recovery, healthy friendships replace toxic influences. They become a source of encouragement, laughter, and truth. Good friends sharpen your character and remind you who you're becoming.

How to Practice This Daily:
• Be the kind of friend you want to have.
• Keep confidences; don't gossip.
• Encourage someone struggling in their journey.
• Show up and listen without judgment.
• Spend time with people who push you toward God, not away.

Reflection Questions:

How have my friendships changed since beginning recovery?

_____

_____

What makes a friendship healthy and Christ-centered?

_____

_____

Who can I encourage or pray for today?

_____

_____

Bible Connection:

Jesus called His followers friends — because love and truth define friendship.
"A friend loves at all times." — Proverbs 17:17 (NIV)

Rate yourself 1–5 daily (1 = Never, 2 = Rarely, 3 = Sometimes, 4 = Often, 5 = Always)

Question	Mon	Tue	Wed	Thu	Fri	Sat	Sun
I was a trustworthy friend today.							
I encouraged someone who was struggling.							
I kept confidences shared with me.							
Weekly Average:							

Why is trustworthy an important moral value to me?

_____

11. Hard Work

Definition: Giving your best effort even when you don't feel like it.
Examples:

- Completing assigned chores without complaining.
- Staying consistent at your job or duties.
- Finishing what you start.
  Reflection: "Whatever you do, work at it with all your heart, as working for the Lord." — *Colossians 3:23 (NIV)*

Why This Matters:
Hard work rebuilds discipline, pride, and purpose. In addiction, we looked for shortcuts and escapes. Recovery teaches perseverance. Each time we give our best, we strengthen our confidence and prepare for life beyond the program. Work becomes worship when it's done with the right heart.

How to Practice This Daily:
• Show up early and ready to serve.
• Finish every task completely.
• Look for ways to go the extra mile.
• Keep a positive attitude even in hard jobs.
• Treat all work as a way to honor God.

Reflection Questions:

How does hard work shape my self-respect?

_____

_____

What excuses have I used to avoid effort in the past?

_____

_____

How can I serve God through my work today?

_____

_____

Bible Connection:
God created us to work with joy and purpose. Every task done faithfully brings Him glory.
"Whatever you do, work at it with all your heart, as working for the Lord." — Colossians 3:23 (NIV)

Rate yourself 1–5 daily (1 = Never, 2 = Rarely, 3 = Sometimes, 4 = Often, 5 = Always)

Question	Mon	Tue	Wed	Thu	Fri	Sat	Sun
I gave my best effort to each task today.							
I finished what I started.							
I kept a positive attitude toward my work.							
Weekly Average:							

Why is Hard work an important moral value to me?

_____

12. Service

Definition: Using your time and gifts to bless others without expecting anything in return.
Examples:

- Helping new residents adjust.
- Volunteering at church or outreach events.
- Doing something kind anonymously.
  Reflection: "The greatest among you will be your servant." — *Matthew 23:11 (NIV)*

Why This Matters:
Service is love in action. It takes the focus off "me" and puts it on helping others. In giving, we receive healing; in serving, we find meaning. Every act of service — big or small — teaches humility, gratitude, and compassion.

How to Practice This Daily:
• Help a new resident settle in.
• Volunteer for extra chores without being asked.
• Offer to pray with or for someone.
• Find small ways to give back every day.
• Serve with joy, not for recognition.

Reflection Questions:

Who can I serve this week without expecting anything in return?

_____

_____

How has serving others helped me grow?

_____

_____

What does service reveal about my heart?

_____

_____

Bible Connection:

Jesus said greatness comes through serving. When we serve others, we reflect His love to the world. *"The greatest among you will be your servant." — Matthew 23:11 (NIV)*

Rate yourself 1–5 daily (1 = Never, 2 = Rarely, 3 = Sometimes, 4 = Often, 5 = Always)

Question	Mon	Tue	Wed	Thu	Fri	Sat	Sun
I looked for ways to help others.							
I served without expecting reward or praise.							
I brought a helpful attitude to my community.							
Weekly Average:							

Why is Service an important moral value to me?

_____

13. Growth

Definition: Learning from every experience and becoming a better person day by day.
Examples:

- Taking feedback seriously.
- Reading or journaling daily.
- Facing fears instead of running from them.
  Reflection: "He who began a good work in you will carry it on to completion." — *Philippians 1:6 (NIV)*

Why This Matters:
Growth isn't always comfortable, but it's necessary. God uses both victories and setbacks to mature us. True recovery means constant progress — not perfection. When we keep learning, we allow God to keep transforming us.

How to Practice This Daily:
• Journal what you learn from mistakes.
• Ask for feedback from mentors or staff.
• Set weekly personal goals.
• Try something new that stretches your faith.
• Celebrate small victories.

Reflection Questions:

What lesson is God teaching me right now?

_____

_____

How do I react to correction or challenge?

_____

_____

What step can I take this week to grow in maturity?

_____

_____

Bible Connection:
Growth is proof of life. God promises to finish what He started in you.
"He who began a good work in you will carry it on to completion." — Philippians 1:6 (NIV)

Rate yourself 1–5 daily (1 = Never, 2 = Rarely, 3 = Sometimes, 4 = Often, 5 = Always)

Question	Mon	Tue	Wed	Thu	Fri	Sat	Sun
I learned from a mistake today.							
I listened to feedback and used it to improve.							
I challenged myself to grow spiritually or mentally.							
Weekly Average:							

Why is growth an important moral value to me?

_____

14. Peace

Definition: Living with inner calm that comes from trusting God, not your circumstances.
Examples:

- Walking away from drama instead of engaging.
- Praying before reacting in anger.
- Letting go of control and surrendering outcomes.
  Reflection: "The peace of God, which surpasses all understanding, will guard your hearts." — *Philippians 4:7 (ESV)*

Why This Matters:
Before recovery, chaos ruled our lives. We reacted instead of responding. Peace comes when we stop fighting everything and start trusting God. It's not the absence of trouble — it's the presence of Christ within us.

How to Practice This Daily:
• Start and end your day in prayer.
• Take deep breaths and pause before reacting.
• Walk away from gossip and drama.
• Forgive quickly to protect your peace.
• Create quiet moments with God daily.

Reflection Questions:

What usually robs me of peace?

_____

_____

How can I protect my peace today?

_____

_____

How does peace help me handle difficult situations differently?

_____

_____

Bible Connection:
Jesus calmed storms with His presence. That same peace can guard your heart.
"The peace of God, which surpasses all understanding, will guard your hearts and minds in Christ Jesus." — Philippians 4:7 (ESV)

Rate yourself 1–5 daily (1 = Never, 2 = Rarely, 3 = Sometimes, 4 = Often, 5 = Always)

Question	Mon	Tue	Wed	Thu	Fri	Sat	Sun
I chose to walk away from drama or arguments.							
I prayed before reacting in anger or stress.							
I made choices that protected my peace today.							
Weekly Average:							

Why is Peace an important moral value to me?

_____

15. Joy

Definition: A deep sense of gladness that doesn't depend on outside situations.
Examples:

- Smiling even through a hard day.
- Celebrating small victories in recovery.
- Choosing to see God's goodness around you.
  Reflection: "The joy of the Lord is my strength." — *Nehemiah 8:10 (KJV)*

Why This Matters:
Joy is not a feeling — it's a choice. It grows when we stay thankful and connected to God, even in hard times. Joy gives strength when life feels heavy and reminds us that victory is found in Christ, not in comfort.

How to Practice This Daily:
• Smile and encourage others with positive words.
• Focus on what's good instead of what's missing.
• Worship and praise God even on tough days.
• Celebrate progress, not perfection.
• Bring laughter and hope into your community.

Reflection Questions:

What's the difference between happiness and joy?

_____

_____

How can I find joy even in challenges?

_____

_____

What moment recently brought me true joy in recovery?

_____

_____

Bible Connection:
Joy is a fruit of the Spirit — it strengthens you to persevere with hope.
"The joy of the Lord is my strength." — Nehemiah 8:10 (KJV)

Rate yourself 1–5 daily (1 = Never, 2 = Rarely, 3 = Sometimes, 4 = Often, 5 = Always)

Question	Mon	Tue	Wed	Thu	Fri	Sat	Sun
I found something good to be thankful for today.							
I shared encouragement or a smile with someone.							
I chose joy even when my circumstances were hard.							
Weekly Average:							

Why is Joy an important moral value to me?

_____

My TOP 5 values I want to build are:

1. _____

2. _____

3. _____

4. _____

5. _____

Why are these values important to me?

_____

_____

PART C: COMMITMENT

8. I commit to focusing on these 3 values this month:

1. _____

2. _____

3. _____

"Learning to Measure My Character"

When we've lived in survival mode, we stop measuring life by what's right and start measuring by what feels good. The Moral Inventory Checklist is a way to begin *measuring again* — not by guilt or shame, but by growth.

Each day you track your honesty, responsibility, respect, and integrity, etc. You are re-training your conscience. This is how we rebuild trust — one truthful day at a time, one responsible choice at a time.

Reflection Verse: "Let us examine our ways and test them, let us return to the Lord." — *Lamentations 3:40 (NIV)*

Think About: What does it mean to be honest with myself? What small area of my life needs more consistency?

WEEKLY REFLECTION

1. Which value did I practice best this week?

_____

2. Which value needs the most work?

_____

3. Specific example of when I acted according to my values:

_____

_____

4. Specific example of when I fell short:

_____

_____

5. What will I do differently next week?

_____

_____

_____

VALUES IN ACTION - SCENARIO PRACTICE

SCENARIO RESPONSES *For each scenario, write how your values would guide your response.*

SCENARIO 1: THE MESSY ROOMMATE

Your roommate consistently leaves messes in the common areas and never cleans up after himself.

Which values apply here?

□ Respect □ Responsibility □ Compassion □ Honesty □ Other: _____

My value-based response would be:

_____

_____

What would my OLD response have been?

_____

_____

SCENARIO 2: LATE FOR WORK

You overslept and are going to be 30 minutes late for work. Your boss has warned you about punctuality before.

Which values apply here?

□ Honesty □ Responsibility □ Integrity □ Humility □ Other: _____

My value-based response would be:

_____

_____

What would my OLD response have been?

_____

_____

SCENARIO 3: PERSONAL SHARING

During group, someone shares something very personal and painful about their past.

Which values apply here?

□ Compassion □ Respect □ Integrity □ Humility □ Other: _____

My value-based response would be:

_____

_____

SCENARIO 4: WANTING TO QUIT

You're having a really hard day and want to leave the program. You're thinking about packing your bags.

Which values apply here?

□ Responsibility □ Integrity □ Faith □ Humility □ Other: _____

My value-based response would be:

_____

_____

What would my OLD response have been?

_____

_____

SCENARIO 5: MONEY TEMPTATION

You find a $20 bill on the floor in the hallway. No one is around and no one saw you pick it up.

Which values apply here?

□ Honesty □ Integrity □ Respect □ Other: _____

My value-based response would be:

_____

_____

What would my OLD response have been?

_____

_____

GROUP DISCUSSION NOTES

1. Which scenario was hardest for you? Why?

_____

_____

2. How do your values conflict with your old thinking?

_____

_____

3. What did you learn from others' responses?

_____

_____

"Daily Renewal"

The daily check-in is more than a habit — it's a moment of renewal. Each evening you stop, reflect, and thank God, you are rewiring your heart.

The more you notice your growth, the more aware you become of God's grace at work in you. Gratitude turns small steps into miracles.

Reflection Verse: "Search me, O God, and know my heart… and lead me in the way everlasting." — *Psalm 139:23–24*
Think About: Where did I see God's hand today? What value am I most thankful to have practiced?

DAILY VALUE CHECK-IN

Complete this each evening before bed.

MONDAY

What value did I practice well today? _____

Example: _____

Where did I fall short of my values? _____

Example: _____

How can I do better tomorrow? _____

Do I need to make amends to anyone? □ Yes □ No If yes, to whom and for what?

_____

Tonight I'm grateful for: _____

TUESDAY

What value did I practice well today? _____

Example: _____

Where did I fall short of my values? _____

Example: _____

How can I do better tomorrow? _____

Do I need to make amends to anyone? □ Yes □ No If yes, to whom and for what?

_____

Tonight I'm grateful for: _____

WEDNESDAY

What value did I practice well today? _____

Example: _____

Where did I fall short of my values? _____

Example: _____

How can I do better tomorrow? _____

Do I need to make amends to anyone? □ Yes □ No If yes, to whom and for what?

_____

Tonight I'm grateful for: _____

THURSDAY

What value did I practice well today? _____

Example: _____

Where did I fall short of my values? _____

Example: _____

How can I do better tomorrow? _____

Do I need to make amends to anyone? □ Yes □ No If yes, to whom and for what?

_____

Tonight I'm grateful for: _____

FRIDAY

What value did I practice well today? _____

Example: _____

Where did I fall short of my values? _____

Example: _____

How can I do better tomorrow? _____

Do I need to make amends to anyone? □ Yes □ No If yes, to whom and for what?

_____

Tonight I'm grateful for: _____

SATURDAY

What value did I practice well today? _____

Example: _____

Where did I fall short of my values? _____

Example: _____

How can I do better tomorrow? _____

Do I need to make amends to anyone? □ Yes □ No If yes, to whom and for what?

_____

Tonight I'm grateful for: _____

SUNDAY

What value did I practice well today? _____

Example: _____

Where did I fall short of my values? _____

Example: _____

How can I do better tomorrow? _____

Do I need to make amends to anyone? □ Yes □ No If yes, to whom and for what?

_____

Tonight I'm grateful for: _____

WEEKLY REFLECTION

This week my strongest value was: _____

This week I need to work on: _____

One thing I learned about myself: _____

Next week I will focus on: _____

"Walking Forward in Freedom"

Living by moral values is not a one-time lesson — it's a lifelong walk. Every day you'll face choices that test what you've learned. But now, you have something powerful: awareness, direction, and God's Spirit inside you.

Keep your moral compass tuned by staying honest, humble, and grateful. The same God who began this work in you will be faithful to finish it.

Reflection Verse: "He has shown you, O man, what is good; and what does the Lord require of you but to do justly, to love mercy, and to walk humbly with your God?" — *Micah 6:8*

Think About: How will I carry these values into the next chapter of my life?

Step 4

Practical Guide – How to Do the Inventory

A) Prepare Well

Preparation Steps- This inventory is designed to be written out on separate notebook.
Pray Psalm 139:23–24
Choose a quiet, safe space and a time block (60–90 minutes).
Have your mentor/sponsor or PRSS identified for support.
Agree to a confidentiality covenant if you're in a group.
Keep water, tissues, a Bible, and grounding tools nearby. Grounding tools: • 5 slow breaths • Name 5 things you see • Feel feet on floor • Brief walk • Drink water • Short prayer

B) The Core Sections

1. Resentments – Who/What I'm Angry At and Why

Person / Situation	What Happened (facts)	How it Affected Me	My Part (if any)	Defects / Patterns	God's Value to Embrace
Boss fired me	I missed shifts while using	Fear (money), shame (identity)	I lied & no-showed	Dishonesty, denial	Truth, responsibility

The following questions are to be used to help you write out your moral inventory:

Questions:

• Who do I resent?

• What promises were broken?

• What story do I tell myself about this?

• Where did I contribute (if at all)?

Note: In childhood abuse, you likely had no part.

2. Fears – And the Behaviors They Drive

Fear	Where it Came From	How I Coped	Cost	Truth to Replace
Being abandoned	Early family chaos	Cling, use, people-please	Toxic ties, relapse	"I will never leave you" (Heb. 13:5)

The following questions are to be used to help you write out your moral inventory:

Questions:

• What am I afraid of (past, present, or future)?

• When fear speaks, what do I do?

• How has fear controlled my decisions?

• Where do I need to trust God instead of fear?

• What's the true Scripture-anchored statement?

3. Harms I've Done to Others

Who	Nature of Harm	Motive / Defect	Living Amends (Step 8 Preview)
Sister	Borrowed $$, never repaid	Selfishness, entitlement	Repay w/ plan & integrity

The following questions are to be used to help you write out your moral inventory:

Questions:

• Where have I harmed others sexually, emotionally, financially, or spiritually?

• How have I manipulated, controlled, or used people?

• How have I failed to love as Christ calls me to love?

4. Harms Done to Me – Trauma Inventory

Who / What	What Happened (brief)	Impact (beliefs formed)	Coping I Adopted	What I Needed Then	Care Plan Now
Older cousin	Boundary violation	"I'm unsafe/dirty"	Numb/act out	Protection, truth	Therapist consult; safe boundaries; prayer for healing

⚠ Important: Writing "Harms Received" is about naming truth and getting care. It is not blaming yourself. Forgiveness is a process, not forced.

5. Harms Done to Self

Pattern	How I Harmed Myself	Defect / Lie	New Value / Practice
Binge using	Health & hope damaged	"I deserve relief now"	Self-control; support calls

4. Relationships & Sexual Conduct Patterns

Questions:

• Where did I use people for comfort/control?

• Where did I tolerate harm?

• What boundaries and God-honoring practices do I need?

7. Secrets & Shame (Never Spoken)

Write it. Name it. Invite God's mercy here first. Shame loses power in the light (1 John 1:7).

Questions:

• What secrets am I still hiding?

• Where do I struggle with dishonesty or self-deception?

• What areas of shame or guilt do I need to face and confess?

8. Character Defects

Questions:

• Which sins or patterns keep showing up (pride, envy, lust, greed, sloth, anger, gluttony, selfishness)?

• How have these defects affected my choices and relationships?

• Which ones am I still holding onto?

9. Moral Values Inventory – Exchange Old for New

My Survival Value & Payoff	God's Value	Practice This Week
Control (feel safe)	Trust / Submission	Surrender prayer AM/PM; share plan with mentor
Image (look good)	Truth	Tell one hard truth promptly
Instant relief	Patience / Sobriety	24-hr rule; call before acting

10. Assets & Graces – Don't Skip This!

List strengths God's already growing—courage to get help, honesty today, protectiveness for family, work ethic, generosity. Healing builds fastest when we name both defects and grace.

Examples to Guide You

Resentment example:

"I resent my ex for 'ruining my life.' Truth: my using, lying, and disappearing ruined trust. Effects: shame, isolation. My part: I broke promises. Defects: dishonesty, selfishness. God's value: truth, humility. Practice: weekly honesty check-in; repay what I can."

Fear example:

"Fear of failure → procrastinate, then use to numb anxiety. Cost: lost jobs. Truth: 'God is able to make all grace abound…' (2 Cor. 9:8). Practice: small tasks daily; text mentor when stuck."

Harm I've done example:

"I harmed a close friend financially by borrowing money and never repaying it. My part: selfishness and greed. Amends: Repay with a plan and integrity."

Harm received example:

"Childhood ridicule → belief 'I'm worthless' → performance & substances. Care plan: therapy consult; memorize Psalm 139:14; boundaries with mocking family member."

When to Pause & Get Help

Flashbacks, panic, suicidal thoughts, desire to harm self/others → Stop, call your mentor/PRSS or licensed therapist immediately. You are not alone.

Confidentiality Covenant (Group Use)

"What's shared here stays here. We honor each other by listening without fixing, advising, or gossiping. We tell the truth and we keep it safe."

Long-Term Reflection – Step 4

Looking back, I see that Step 4 was one of the hardest things I ever did — but also one of the most freeing. Writing down my resentments, fears, and defects helped me stop pretending and start living honestly.

Over the years, I've had to revisit Step 4 more than once. Each time, God showed me something new. Step 4 taught me that honesty isn't just for the beginning of recovery — it's a way of life.

I have learned so much about myself over the years by taking multiple 4th Step Inventories. Each time, I become a little more honest, and I can see things about myself that I wasn't able to see in years prior.

STEP 5

We admitted to God, to ourselves, and to another human being the exact nature of our wrongs.

Scripture Foundation

"Therefore confess your sins to each other and pray for each other so that you may be healed." (James 5:16) (NIV)

"If we confess our sins, he is faithful and just and will forgive us our sins and purify us from all unrighteousness." (1 John 1:9) (NIV)

"Whoever conceals their sins does not prosper, but the one who confesses and renounces them finds mercy." (Proverbs 28:13) (NIV)

Introduction – The Healing Power of Confession

Step 5 is where the inventory of Step 4 comes alive. Writing our moral inventory was a courageous act, but now we must take the next step: admitting it.

Confession breaks the power of secrecy and shame. When we bring our wrongs into the light—to God, to ourselves, and to another trusted person—healing begins. This step is not about humiliation; it is about freedom.

This is where the weight begins to lift. Secrets lose their power when brought into the light. Confession is not about punishment; it's about healing. Step 5 asks us to be vulnerable in three directions, and each direction serves a unique purpose in our recovery.

James 5:16 (NIV) tells us, *"Therefore confess your sins to each other and pray for each other so that you may be healed."* Confession is God's pathway to healing. It strips shame of its power and opens the door to grace.

Teaching & Lesson Content

1. Three Directions of Confession

Step 5 calls us to confess in three directions, and each one is essential:

To God (For Forgiveness):

God already knows everything we've done, but confession is not for His information—it's for our transformation. When we confess to God, we agree with His truth about our sin and receive His forgiveness. 1 John 1:9 (NIV) promises, *"If we confess our sins, he is faithful and just and will forgive us our sins and purify us from all unrighteousness."*

To Ourselves (For Honesty):

Many of us have spent years lying to ourselves, minimizing our wrongs, or blaming others. Step 5 requires us to be brutally honest with ourselves. We must stop making excuses and accept the truth: "This is who I was, but it is not who I have to remain."

To Another Person (For Accountability and Healing):

Confessing to another human being breaks the isolation that shame creates. When we speak our secrets out loud to someone we trust, we discover that we are not alone and that grace is real. The other person becomes a witness to God's mercy and a reminder that we are loved despite our failures.

2. Breaking Isolation

Secrets keep us sick; confession opens the door to freedom. The enemy thrives in secrecy. He wants us to believe that if anyone really knew us, they would reject us. But Step 5 proves that lie wrong.

When we confess to another person and they respond with grace instead of condemnation, we experience the love of God in a tangible way. We realize that we are not defined by our worst moments. Confession breaks the chains of isolation and invites us into community and accountability.

3. The Root Causes

Step 5 is where patterns and defects are uncovered and named. As we confess, we begin to see the deeper issues behind our behaviors—pride, lust, envy, greed, anger, fear, selfishness. These are the root causes that drove our actions.

Naming these defects is not about condemnation; it's about clarity. Once we can name what's been controlling us, we can begin to surrender it to God. Step 5 helps us move from surface-level confession ("I did this") to deeper understanding ("I did this because of pride, fear, or selfishness").

4. Trust and Discernment

Choosing the right person to hear our Step 5 is crucial. This should be someone who:

- Is trustworthy and will keep your confession confidential.
- Understands recovery and the 12 steps.
- Will listen without judgment or condemnation.
- Can offer grace, encouragement, and accountability.

Common choices include a sponsor, mentor, pastor, counselor, or trusted recovery partner. Do not choose someone who will gossip, shame you, or use your confession against you. Pray and ask God to guide you to the right person.

5. Why Confession Heals

Confession heals because it brings truth into the light. Shame grows in darkness, but it withers in the light of honesty. When we speak our secrets out loud, we strip them of their power.

Confession also aligns us with God's truth. It says, "I was wrong. I take responsibility. I need God's grace." This humility opens the door for God to work in us and through us.

Proverbs 28:13 (NIV) *"Whoever conceals their sins does not prosper, but the one who confesses and renounces them finds mercy."* Confession is the pathway to mercy, healing, and freedom.

Story Box – My Personal Journey

When I prepared to share my Step 5, I was terrified. I thought if someone really knew everything I had done, they would walk away. I had spent so many years hiding behind lies, excuses, and denial. The idea of speaking the truth out loud felt like stepping off a cliff.

But when I confessed, I found grace instead of rejection. My mentor didn't excuse my wrongs, but he reminded me of God's forgiveness. He listened without judgment and spoke words of encouragement and hope. Speaking those words out loud broke chains of shame that had bound me for years.

I realized that God's love was greater than my darkest secrets. Step 5 became a turning point where guilt began to lift and healing began to grow. For the first time, I felt truly free—not because I was perfect, but because I had been honest and received grace.

Over the years, I've learned that confession is not just a one-time event. It's a lifestyle. Whenever I fail, I've discovered the quickest path to freedom is to admit it—first to God, then to myself, then to someone I trust. Step 5 taught me that the enemy's greatest weapon is secrecy. Once my wrongs are spoken, their power is broken. The freedom I found in this step continues to remind me that honesty is the path to healing.

Step 5 Practical Guide – How to Share Your Moral Inventory

Step-by-Step Instructions

1. Admit to God

- Pray through what you've written in your Step 4 inventory.
- Tell God honestly: *"Lord, this is what I've done. This is who I've been. Forgive me and change me."*
- Remember 1 John 1:9 (NIV) *"If we confess our sins, He is faithful and just to forgive us our sins and purify us from all unrighteousness."*
- Don't rush. Take time to confess each area thoroughly.

2. Admit to Yourself

- Read your inventory out loud to yourself before sharing it with someone else.
- Hearing your own words makes the truth more real.
- Accept: "This is who I was, but it is not who I have to remain."
- Stop making excuses or minimizing. Own the truth fully.

3. Admit to Another Person

- Choose a safe person: sponsor, mentor, pastor, or trusted recovery partner.
- Schedule a time when you won't be rushed or interrupted.
- Be thorough. Don't hide or edit—partial confession still leaves chains intact.
- Let them listen. You don't need advice at every turn; what you need is to be heard and accepted.
- Trust that God already knows and forgives; this step brings you into agreement with His truth.

Tips for Sharing Honestly

- **Don't sugarcoat or minimize.** Say it plainly.
- **Don't justify:** "I did this because they hurt me." Own your part.
- **Don't rush**—take the time to be thorough.
- **Be specific.** Instead of "I was dishonest," say "I lied to my boss about being sick when I was hungover."
- **Trust the process.** Confession may feel uncomfortable, but it leads to freedom.

Example Confessions

Example 1 – Family Resentment:

"I resented my father for abandoning us. I blamed him for my drinking. The truth is, I used that resentment as an excuse to numb my pain. My root cause was resentment and fear of rejection."

Example 2 – Dishonesty at Work:

"I lied to my boss and said I was sick when I was hungover. I felt guilty but kept doing it. My defect was dishonesty and laziness. I'm ashamed because it showed I couldn't be trusted."

Example 3 – Infidelity in a Relationship:

"I cheated on someone I loved. I justified it by saying they didn't care, but the truth is, I was selfish and lustful. My defect was lust and ego. I still carry shame that I wasn't faithful."

Example 4 – Financial Harm:

"I borrowed money from my sister and never paid her back. I told myself I would eventually, but I spent it on drugs instead. My defect was selfishness and greed. I damaged our relationship and her trust."

Reflection Questions

What fears do I have about sharing my Step 5?

_____

_____

_____

Who is a trustworthy person I can choose to hear my confession?

_____

_____

_____

What do I hope will happen when I admit the truth?

_____

_____

_____

How might confession bring healing, not just guilt?

_____

_____

_____

Which areas of my inventory feel the hardest to confess? Why?

_____

_____

_____

What would it mean to experience grace instead of condemnation?

_____

_____

_____

Reflection After Confession

How did it feel to speak your secrets out loud?

_____

_____

_____

Did you experience relief, fear, or both?

_____

_____

_____

What did you hear from the other person that encouraged you?

_____

_____

_____

Which areas still feel heavy, and need more surrender to God?

_____

_____

_____

What has changed in how you see yourself after confession?

_____

_____

_____

Practical Application

- Schedule a time with your mentor or sponsor to share your Step 5.
- Pray before beginning: *"Lord, give me the courage to tell the truth and the humility to receive grace."*
- Write down how you feel afterward—what emotions surfaced, and what peace followed.
- Thank the person who listened to your Step 5 for their time, grace, and support.

Choice Point – Step 5

I can either stay chained by secrecy, or I can step into the light of freedom.

- Will I keep hiding behind shame, or will I confess my wrongs?
- Will I cling to pride, or will I humble myself before God and others?
- Will I continue to carry the weight of my secrets, or will I trust God's grace to set me free?

Today, I choose truth—to admit my wrongs and walk in healing. I choose to trust that God's love is greater than my darkest secrets.

Long-Term Reflection – Step 5

Over the years, I've learned that confession is not just a one-time event. It's a lifestyle. Whenever I fail, I've discovered the quickest path to freedom is to admit it—first to God, then to myself, then to someone I trust.

Step 5 taught me that the enemy's greatest weapon is secrecy. Once my wrongs are spoken, their power is broken. The freedom I found in this step continues to remind me that honesty is the path to healing.

I've also learned that confession doesn't just free me from the past—it protects my future. When I practice regular confession and accountability, I'm less likely to fall back into old patterns. Honesty becomes a way of life, and grace becomes my daily experience.

Looking back, Step 5 was one of the most terrifying and liberating steps I've ever taken. It taught me that I don't have to hide anymore. I can live in the light, knowing that God's love and grace are greater than anything I've ever done.

Closing Prayer

"Lord, thank You for giving me the courage to confess. Thank You that You do not condemn me but forgive me. I ask You to take what I have confessed and remove its power over my life. Help me to walk in honesty, humility, and freedom, one day at a time. Thank You for Your grace that is greater than all my sin. Amen."

STEP 6

We were entirely ready to have God remove all these defects of character.

Scripture Foundation

"Humble yourselves before the Lord, and He will lift you up." (James 4:10) (NIV)

"Create in me a pure heart, O God, and renew a steadfast spirit within me." (Psalm 51:10) (NIV)

"Therefore, if anyone is in Christ, the new creation has come: The old has gone, the new is here!" (2 Corinthians 5:17) (NIV)

Introduction – Readiness for Change

Step 6 is about willingness. After writing our inventory (Step 4) and confessing it (Step 5), we now face the reality of our character defects. Pride, fear, lust, anger, envy, greed, selfishness, they all rise to the surface.

But here's the challenge: are we ready to let them go? God will not force transformation on us. He respects our free will. Step 6 asks: Am I willing to release these defects, or am I still clinging to them?

After honestly facing our past and confessing it, we now stand at the crossroads: Am I truly willing to let God remove these defects, or am I still holding onto them? This step reminds us that recovery is not about behavior modifications; it's about heart transformation.

Character defects are often comfortable; they have been our coping tools, our shields, our excuses. Letting them go requires humility and trust. Step 6 is not about perfection or pretending our defects are gone. It's about recognizing them when they appear, naming them, and being willing to let them go—again and again.

Teaching & Lesson Content

1. Defects Identified

Character defects are the attitudes and behaviors that repeatedly lead us to sin. They are the patterns we identified in Step 4—the roots beneath our destructive actions.

Common defects include:

- **Pride** – thinking we're better than others or refusing to admit we're wrong.
- **Fear** – letting anxiety control our decisions.
- **Dishonesty** – lying to ourselves and others.
- **Selfishness** – putting our needs above everyone else's.
- **Lust** – using people for our own gratification.
- **Anger** – lashing out or holding resentment.
- **Envy** – resenting others for what they have.
- **Greed** – always wanting more, never satisfied.

These defects didn't develop overnight, and they won't disappear overnight. But Step 6 prepares us to surrender them to God.

2. The Illusion of Control

We cannot "manage" our defects any better than we could manage our addiction. Just as we were powerless over substances, we are powerless over our character defects. We cannot fix ourselves through willpower or self-improvement.

The good news is that we don't have to. God is the one who removes defects. Our job is simply to be willing—to stop protecting them, excusing them, or clinging to them.

3. Willingness Is the Key

God removes what we are ready to release, but not what we cling to. This is the heart of Step 6. We must become "entirely ready"—not partially ready, not ready for some defects but not others. Entirely ready.

But here's the truth: many of us aren't ready. We secretly enjoy some of our defects. Pride makes us feel superior. Anger gives us a sense of power. Lust offers temporary pleasure. Fear keeps us from taking risks that might lead to failure.

Step 6 asks us to be honest: What defects am I still holding onto? What am I afraid will happen if God removes them? Who will I be without these familiar patterns?

If you're not ready, that's okay. Pray for willingness. Ask God to make you ready. Even the desire to be willing is a starting point.

4. Sanctification Is a Process

Sanctification is the process of God making us holy, transforming us into the image of Christ. It is not instant perfection but a lifelong journey. Each time a defect reappears, we must:

1. **Recognize it** – Notice when pride, fear, or anger shows up.
2. **Acknowledge it** – Admit it honestly: "This is happening again."
3. **Ask God to remove it** – Surrender it in prayer: "Lord, take this from me."

Some defects God removes instantly. Others, He removes gradually, layer by layer, as we grow in faith and surrender. The key is daily readiness—a posture of humility that says, "God, I'm willing. Do Your work in me."

5. Daily Readiness

Step 6 is not a one-time readiness; it's a lifelong posture of humility. Every day, we must choose to be ready for God to change us. Every time a defect surfaces, we must choose surrender over self-will.

This is the ongoing work of recovery and discipleship. We don't "graduate" from Step 6. We live in it, day by day, trusting that God is faithful to complete the work He began in us (Philippians 1:6).

Story Box – My Personal Journey

When I first faced Step 6, I thought I was ready for God to remove all my defects. But the truth is, there were some I wasn't ready to give up.

Smoking was one of them. I justified it, minimized it, and tried every way to quit on my own. But God waited until I was truly willing. When I finally surrendered, He delivered me instantly—and I've never smoked again.

Step 6 taught me that real change begins with willingness. God will not rip defects from me against my will. But when I'm ready, He is faithful to remove them.

Over the years, I've learned that Step 6 is not just a checkpoint—it's a lifelong process. New defects surface as life goes on. Each time, I must ask: Am I ready to let this go?

At first, I thought I was only powerless over drugs and alcohol. But as time passed, I realized other defects—pride, fear, envy, selfishness—were just as dangerous if left unchecked. Each time one of these surfaced, I had to come back to Step 6: "Am I ready to let this go?"

What I've discovered is that sanctification—the process of God making me holy—is lifelong. There were seasons where He delivered me instantly, like with smoking and cursing. And there were seasons where I had to keep praying, day after day, for Him to work in me.

The beauty of this process is that I don't have to be discouraged when I see old defects rise up again. Instead, I see them as reminders that God is still working in me. Living this step has taught me that recovery and discipleship both require humility, patience, and daily surrender.

Readiness Guide – Preparing to Let Go

1. List Your Defects

From your Step 4 inventory, identify your key character defects. Write them down clearly:

- Pride
- Fear
- Dishonesty
- Selfishness

- Lust
- Anger
- Envy
- Greed

- Control
- Resentment

2. Ask Yourself

For each defect, ask:

- Am I fully willing to let this go, or am I holding onto it?
- What benefit do I think this defect gives me?
- What am I afraid will happen if God removes it?
- Do I secretly enjoy this defect or use it to protect myself?

3. Pray for Willingness

Even if you're not ready, ask God to make you willing. Pray:

"Lord, I'm not sure I'm ready to let go of [defect], but I want to be ready. Please give me the willingness to surrender this to You. Help me trust that Your way is better than mine."

Reflection Questions

What character defects do I secretly still enjoy or excuse?

_____

_____

_____

Am I afraid of who I'll be without these defects?

_____

_____

_____

Am I truly ready for God to change me, or do I want to stay the same?

_____

_____

_____

What habit or behavior do I know is wrong, but I still cling to?

_____

_____

_____

Which defects keep reappearing in my daily life?

_____

_____

_____

How do I respond when I get triggered?

_____

_____

_____

Am I truly willing to let God take all of my defects, or am I keeping some hidden?

_____

_____

_____

What would my life look like if God removed this defect completely?

_____

_____

_____

Practical Application

- **Daily Prayer of Willingness:** Each morning, pray: *"Lord, today I choose to be ready for You to change me. Make me willing to let go of what keeps me bound."*
- **Write out a prayer of surrender** for each defect, even if you don't yet feel ready.
- **Share your list** with a mentor or sponsor and talk about which defects are hardest to release.
- **Spotting Triggers:** When a defect rises up, pause and ask: "What am I afraid of right now? What need am I trying to meet in an unhealthy way?"
- **Accountability:** Share honestly with a mentor or peer when you see a recurring pattern.

Choice Point – Step 6

I can hold on to my defects, or I can release them into God's hands.

- Will I cling to pride, fear, or lust, or will I be ready to let God remove them?
- Will I excuse my defects, or will I surrender them?
- Will I keep trying to manage them on my own, or will I trust God to transform me?

Today, I choose readiness—to allow God to change my heart. I may not feel ready for everything, but I'm willing to be made willing.

Long-Term Reflection – Step 6

Looking back, I see that Step 6 is not just a checkpoint—it's a lifelong process. New defects surface as life goes on. Each time, I must ask: Am I ready to let this go?

Over the years, I've learned that God is patient. He waits until I am truly willing. And when I surrender, His power is greater than any defect. Step 6 continues to remind me that recovery is not about trying harder—it's about choosing readiness and letting God do what only He can do.

Over the years, I've learned that Steps 6 and 7 are not steps I "completed" once and moved on from. They are steps I return to again and again, because life keeps showing me new layers of my heart that need God's touch.

At first, I thought I was only powerless over drugs and alcohol. But as time passed, I realized other defects—pride, fear, envy, selfishness—were just as dangerous if left unchecked. Each time one of these surfaced, I had to come back to Step 6: "Am I ready to let this go?"

What I've discovered is that sanctification—the process of God making me holy—is lifelong. There were seasons where He delivered me instantly, like with smoking and cursing. And there were seasons where I had to keep praying, day after day, for Him to work in me.

The beauty of this process is that I don't have to be discouraged when I see old defects rise up again. Instead, I see them as reminders that God is still working in me. Living this step has taught me that recovery and discipleship both require humility, patience, and daily surrender.

Readiness is not a feeling—it's a choice. And every day, I choose to be ready for God to continue His transforming work in me.

Closing Prayer

"Lord, I confess that I am not perfect and that I still struggle with character defects. I ask You to make me entirely ready to let them go. Where I am unwilling, make me willing. Where I am afraid, give me courage. Where I am clinging, help me release. Create in me a pure heart, O God, and renew a steadfast spirit within me. I trust that You are faithful to complete the work You have begun in me. Amen."

STEP 7

We humbly asked Him to remove our shortcomings.

Scripture Foundation

"Humble yourselves before the Lord, and He will lift you up." (James 4:10) (NIV)

"God opposes the proud but gives grace to the humble." (1 Peter 5:5) (NIV)

"Create in me a pure heart, O God, and renew a steadfast spirit within me." (Psalm 51:10) (NIV)

Introduction – The Step of Humility

Step 7 is where willingness becomes prayer. After becoming ready in Step 6, now we humbly ask God to remove our defects.

Humility is the heart of this step. We cannot demand God's power; we can only ask in surrender. Shortcomings are not erased through willpower but through God's transforming grace. Step 7 is where we bow before Him and invite His Spirit to do the work we cannot do ourselves.

If Step 6 is about readiness, Step 7 is about humility. We confess that we cannot remove these defects by our own willpower. Only God can do this work in us. Humility is not self-hatred; it is honesty about our dependence on God. It is the daily, sometimes moment-by-moment choice to surrender again.

Some defects God removes instantly; others He reshapes slowly, teaching us patience and dependence. Living Step 7 means asking humbly—not demanding, not bargaining—and trusting God's timing.

Teaching & Lesson Content

1. From Readiness to Request

Step 6 prepared our hearts; Step 7 turns that readiness into prayer. We move from "I'm willing" to "Lord, please do this work in me."

This is not a passive step. It requires action—the action of humbling ourselves and asking God for help. We acknowledge that we have tried to fix ourselves and failed. Now we turn to the only One who can truly change us.

2. Humility Defined

Humility is not weakness, and it's not thinking less of ourselves. Humility is recognizing our complete dependence on God. It's admitting: "I need You. I cannot do this on my own. Without You, I will fall back into the same patterns."

Humility is also honesty. It means we stop pretending we have it all together. We stop trying to impress others or maintain an image. We come before God as we truly are—broken, needy, and desperate for His grace.

James 4:10 (NIV) promises, *"Humble yourselves before the Lord, and He will lift you up."* When we humble ourselves, God lifts us. When we admit our weakness, He shows His strength.

3. God's Timing

Some defects are removed instantly; others fade through a lifelong process. We don't get to choose which ones or when. That's part of humility—trusting God's timing and methods.

There may be defects you've prayed about for years that God hasn't removed yet. That doesn't mean He isn't working. Sometimes God uses the struggle to teach us patience, dependence, and deeper faith. Other times, He waits until we're truly ready to let go.

And then there are the moments of grace—when God removes a defect instantly, miraculously, without explanation. Those moments remind us that He is powerful and that He loves us.

4. Partnership with Grace

God does the removing, but we cooperate through obedience. Step 7 is not a magic prayer that makes everything disappear. It's an invitation into partnership with God.

He removes the defect, but we must walk in obedience. If God is working to remove dishonesty, we must practice telling the truth. If He's removing selfishness, we must practice serving others. If He's removing lust, we must guard our eyes and hearts.

Grace empowers us, but obedience demonstrates our willingness. We pray, "Lord, remove this," and then we live as if He is doing exactly that.

5. Living Step 7 Daily

Step 7 is not a one-time prayer—it's a rhythm of life. Every time a defect resurfaces, we return to humility and ask God again. We don't give up. We don't get discouraged. We simply keep asking, keep surrendering, keep trusting.

This is the lifelong process of sanctification—God making us holy, one layer at a time. Some days we see progress. Other days, we feel like we're back at square one. But God is faithful. He who began a good work in us will carry it on to completion (Philippians 1:6).

Story Box – My Personal Journey

When I prayed my first Step 7 prayer, I honestly didn't expect much. But I remember the day God removed my desire to smoke after years of trying. I had prayed about it countless times before—but when I truly surrendered, He delivered me instantly. I never smoked again.

Other defects, like pride or selfishness, have taken much longer. Step 7 taught me that God's power is greater than mine, but His timing and methods are His own. My part is to remain humble, ask honestly, and trust Him.

One of the reasons I love Psalm 51:10 is because it was and is God who cleans my heart. My testimony is that He has done this in many areas of my life. When I surrendered, God delivered me from drugs and alcohol. He took away my desire to curse. These were not changes I made on my own—they were acts of His mercy and grace.

I came to understand that my part was to be willing, to ask humbly, and to trust His timing. Some defects left quickly, like the day He removed my craving for cigarettes. Others took time, requiring me to pray daily, "Lord, please take this from me."

Step 7 taught me that it is God who renews, God who cleanses, and God who restores. My role is to stay humble, honest, and willing—one day at a time.

Over the years, I've discovered that Step 7 is not a one-time prayer—it's a rhythm of life. Every time a defect resurfaces, I return to humility and ask God again. Step 7 reminds me daily that transformation is God's work, not mine. My job is to stay humble, stay honest, and keep asking. The more I surrender, the more I see His power at work in me.

Step 7 Prayer Guide

The Step 7 Prayer

"My Creator, I am now willing that You should have all of me, good and bad. I pray that You now remove from me every single defect of character which stands in the way of my usefulness to You and my fellows. Grant me strength, as I go out from here, to do Your bidding. Amen."

How to Pray Step 7

1. **Admit Need** – "Lord, I cannot remove this defect on my own. I have tried and failed."
2. **Ask Humbly** – "I ask You to remove it in Your time and in Your way. I trust Your wisdom and Your love."
3. **Trust His Timing** – "Whether You deliver me instantly or gradually, I trust You. I will not give up."
4. **Stay Obedient** – "Show me how to walk in Your will as You transform me. Help me cooperate with Your grace."

Praying for Specific Defects

Write out each defect and pray specifically:

"Lord, I humbly ask You to remove my [pride/fear/dishonesty/selfishness/lust/anger]. I cannot do this on my own. I surrender this to You and ask You to transform my heart. Give me the strength to walk in obedience as You work in me. Amen."

Reflection Questions

What shortcomings do I need to bring before God today?

_____

_____

_____

Am I willing to accept His timing and His way of removing them?

_____

_____

_____

Do I see humility as weakness or as strength?

_____

_____

_____

How has God already changed parts of my character?

_____

_____

_____

What does humility look like in my life right now?

_____

_____

_____

How do I feel about asking God for help with the same defect more than once?

_____

_____

_____

Have I experienced God removing a defect or desire from me in a surprising way?

_____

_____

_____

How does living one day at a time help me when I feel discouraged?

_____

_____

_____

Practical Application

- **Humble Prayer:** Pray daily: *"Lord, I cannot change myself. Please remove what stands between me and You."*
- **Write out each defect** and pray specifically for God to remove it.
- **Share one defect** with your mentor or sponsor and ask them to pray with you.
- **Journal any changes** you notice in your heart or behavior after consistent Step 7 prayers.
- **Gratitude List:** Write down examples of defects God has already removed or weakened in your life.
- **Serving Others:** Practice humility by putting someone else's needs above your own this week.

Choice Point – Step 7

I can try to fix myself, or I can humbly ask God to do what I cannot.

- Will I keep relying on my willpower, or will I ask God to remove my defects?
- Will I cling to pride, or will I choose humility?
- Will I demand instant results, or will I trust God's timing?

Today, I choose surrender—to ask God to transform me from the inside out. I choose humility over pride, dependence over self-reliance, and trust over control.

Long-Term Reflection – Step 7

Over the years, I've learned that Steps 6 and 7 are not steps I "completed" once and moved on from. They are steps I return to again and again, because life keeps showing me new layers of my heart that need God's touch.

At first, I thought I was only powerless over drugs and alcohol. But as time passed, I realized other defects—pride, fear, envy, selfishness—were just as dangerous if left unchecked. Each time one of these surfaced, I had to come back to Step 6: "Am I ready to let this go?" and Step 7: "Lord, please take it from me."

What I've discovered is that sanctification—the process of God making me holy—is lifelong. There were seasons where He delivered me instantly, like with smoking and cursing. And there were seasons where I had to keep praying, day after day, for Him to work in me.

The beauty of this process is that I don't have to be discouraged when I see old defects rise up again. Instead, I see them as reminders that God is still working in me. Living this step has taught me that recovery and discipleship both require humility, patience, and daily surrender.

Over the years, I've discovered that Step 7 is not a one-time prayer—it's a rhythm of life. Every time a defect resurfaces, I return to humility and ask God again. Step 7 reminds me daily that transformation is God's work, not mine. My job is to stay humble, stay honest, and keep asking. The more I surrender, the more I see His power at work in me.

I've learned to celebrate the small victories—the moments when I respond with patience instead of anger, when I choose honesty instead of deception, when I serve instead of demanding my own way. These are signs that God is at work, even when the process feels slow.

And I've learned to be patient with myself. Sanctification is not a race. It's a journey. God is not in a hurry, and He doesn't give up on me. Neither should I give up on myself.

Closing Prayer

"My Creator, I am now willing that You should have all of me, good and bad. I pray that You now remove from me every single defect of character which stands in the way of my usefulness to You and my fellows. Grant me strength, as I go out from here, to do Your bidding. I humbly ask You to transform my heart, renew my mind, and make me more like Christ. I trust Your timing, Your methods, and Your love. Thank You for Your patience with me. Amen."

STEP 8

We made a list of all persons we had harmed, and became willing to make amends to them all.

Scripture Foundation

"Do not be deceived: God cannot be mocked. A man reaps what he sows." (Galatians 6:7) (NIV)

"Therefore, if you are offering your gift at the altar and there remember that your brother or sister has something against you, leave your gift there in front of the altar. First go and be reconciled to them; then come and offer your gift." (Matthew 5:23–24) (NIV)

"If it is possible, as far as it depends on you, live at peace with everyone." (Romans 12:18) (NIV)

Introduction – The Ripple Effect of Sin

Step 8 is more than just writing names on a piece of paper. It is about facing the truth that our sin and addiction have never affected just us. Every choice we made created ripples that spread outward—into our families, our friendships, our workplaces, our communities, and even into the next generation.

Addiction often convinces us: "I'm only hurting myself." But the reality is very different. The ripple effect of sin is real, and it grows:

- **Family Damage:** Broken trust, abuse, neglect, financial instability, and emotional wounds.
- **Community Damage:** Crime, lost opportunities, fractured relationships, damaged reputation.
- **Spiritual Damage:** Sin separates us from God and can cause others to stumble in their faith.
- **Generational Damage:** Children often repeat the patterns they see unless someone chooses to break the cycle.

Step 8 calls us to face this reality with honesty—not to shame us, but to prepare us for freedom. This step is the preparation step. Here we don't rush into amends; instead, we prayerfully create our list and become willing to clean up our side of the street.

For many, this list is overwhelming. Years of addiction often left a trail of collateral damage—financial, emotional, physical, spiritual. When we look honestly at the harm caused, it can feel impossible to repair. That's why Step 8 must begin in the hands of Jesus.

The Call of Step 8

This step asks us to look squarely at the damage we have caused—not to condemn ourselves, but to prepare to make things right. It is about cleaning up our side of the street and becoming willing to face the ripple effects of our actions with humility.

This is not about fixing others, pointing out their faults, or demanding their forgiveness. It is about acknowledging our part, becoming willing to make things right, and freeing ourselves from guilt.

This takes prayer, courage, and wise counsel from mentors or sponsors. We don't rush into amends blindly. Instead, we ask God to show us:

- Who to approach.
- When the timing is right.
- How to make an amend that brings healing instead of further harm.

Step 8 is about preparation and willingness. We may not be ready to make all the amends yet, but we must become willing. Willingness is the key that unlocks the door to freedom.

Teaching & Lesson Content

Key Principles of Step 8

1. Prayerful Preparation

Making amends requires prayer, guidance, and counsel from a mentor or sponsor. We don't do this step alone. We need wisdom to know who to approach, what to say, and when the timing is right.

Some amends are straightforward. Others are complex and require careful thought. We must pray over each name on our list and ask God: "Is now the time? How should I approach this? What does healing look like here?"

2. Focus on Self

This is about my part, not the harm others caused me. Step 8 is not the place to point fingers or justify our actions. It's not about saying, "I hurt you, but you hurt me first."

We focus only on our side of the street. We take responsibility for what we did, regardless of what was done to us. This is humility in action.

3. Timing Matters

Some amends must wait until the other person is ready or until God opens the door. Forcing an amend before someone is ready can cause more harm than good.

God's timing is crucial. We may need to wait months or even years before certain amends can be made. In the meantime, we practice living amends—changing our behavior and proving through our actions that we are different.

4. Living Amends

Sometimes direct amends aren't possible—but we can live differently today to show ongoing change. A living amend means that our life becomes the apology. We demonstrate through our actions, over time, that we are not the same person who caused the harm.

Living amends are especially important when:

- The person has passed away.
- The person doesn't want contact with us.
- Making direct amends would cause more harm.

In these cases, we honor the person by living in a way that reflects the change God has made in us.

5. Release of Guilt

The outcome is not about whether others forgive us—it's about becoming free from the weight of our past. We cannot control how others respond. Some will forgive us. Others will reject us. But our freedom comes from doing our part and leaving the results in God's hands.

Step 8 is not about earning forgiveness from others. It's about being obedient to God, taking responsibility for our actions, and releasing the guilt that has kept us in bondage.

Story Box – My Personal Journey

When I first sat down to write my Step 8 list, I thought I was only dealing with a few people. But the more I prayed and reflected, the more I saw how far the damage of my addiction had spread.

I realized I had caused financial harm to people who had trusted me. I had caused emotional pain to family, who had to watch me spiral. I had left behind spiritual wounds in those who doubted God because of the way I lived. And I saw how my children carried scars from choices I made when I was bound by sin.

At first, I was overwhelmed. The list seemed endless. But God reminded me that this step wasn't about fixing everything at once. It was about becoming willing—willing to face the truth, willing to clean up my side of the street, willing to let Him guide me in timing and approach.

When I wrote my Step 8 list, I was overwhelmed. I had left so much collateral damage in people's lives that I thought, "I'll never be able to really make all these amends."

I prayed and asked God to reveal the people who were ready to receive my apology in kindness. Some amends were received with grace—people could see that the real, sober me wasn't the same person who had harmed them. Other amends were rejected harshly, like when I tried to make amends to a family who had lost their son to addiction. They told me to get out of their face and never come back.

I've learned that making amends is not about how the other person reacts. It's about doing my part to clean up my side of the street. God forgave me a long time ago, but Step 8 helped me forgive myself and stop carrying the weight of guilt.

Financial amends took years—over a decade of paying back a lawyer. Family amends were the hardest, because they had been hurt the most and knew my patterns. They tested me to see if I was truly changed. That's why I learned that amends are not just words—they are also living amends that prove through action that I am not the same person I once was.

Some people forgave me quickly. Others wanted nothing to do with me. But the freedom came not from how they responded, but from knowing I had done my part. Step 8 showed me that my sin had rippled out far and wide—but it also showed me that God's grace could ripple even farther, bringing healing where destruction once spread.

Creating Your Step 8 List

Categories of Harm

As you create your list, consider these categories:

Financial Harm:

- Money borrowed and not repaid.
- Theft or fraud.
- Damage to property.
- Lost income due to your actions.

Emotional Harm:

- Lies and broken promises.
- Betrayal and infidelity.
- Neglect and abandonment.
- Verbal abuse or manipulation.

Physical Harm:

- Violence or threats.
- Driving under the influence.
- Endangering others through reckless behavior.

Spiritual Harm:

- Causing others to stumble in their faith.
- Being a poor witness for Christ.
- Leading others into sin or addiction.

Relational Harm:

- Broken trust.
- Damaged friendships.
- Family relationships destroyed.
- Professional relationships ruined.

How to Build Your List

1. **Pray first.** Ask God to reveal the people you've harmed.
2. **Write every name.** Don't edit or justify. Just write.
3. **Include institutions.** Employers, churches, schools, legal systems.
4. **Be specific about the harm.** What did you do? How did it affect them?
5. **Note your part.** What was your role? What were your motives or defects?
6. **Don't include people who harmed you.** This is not the place to address what others did to you.

Reflection Questions

Who in my life has been hurt by my actions?

_____

_____

_____

How has my sin rippled outward into family, friends, community, or future generations?

_____

_____

_____

Am I willing to let God guide me in cleaning up my side of the street?

_____

_____

_____

Am I prepared to leave the outcome in God's hands, no matter how others respond?

_____

_____

_____

Which of these amends seem overwhelming or impossible?

_____

_____

_____

How do I feel about the possibility that some people may never forgive me?

_____

_____

_____

What does it mean for me to "clean up my side of the street"?

_____

_____

_____

Am I willing to let God guide the timing and method of each amend?

_____

_____

_____

Practical Application

- **Start Your List:** Write down every person, place, or institution you harmed. Don't edit yet—just get it all out.
- **Pray Over Each Name:** Ask God, "Is now the time, or should I wait? How should I approach this person?"
- **Seek Counsel:** Review your list with a mentor or sponsor for wisdom and guidance.
- **Be Willing:** Even if amends seem impossible, surrender them to God's timing.
- **Practice Living Amends:** Where direct amends aren't possible, commit to living differently today as evidence of change.

Choice Point – Step 8

I can continue to carry the weight of my past, or I can become willing to make things right.

- Will I face the damage I've caused, or will I continue to hide from it?
- Will I take responsibility for my part, or will I blame others?
- Will I trust God's timing, or will I rush ahead or avoid the work altogether?

Today, I choose willingness. I choose to face the truth, to take responsibility, and to trust God to guide me in making amends.

Long-Term Reflection – Step 8

With time, I've seen that Step 8 is not about checking off a list. It is about developing a lifestyle of accountability and humility.

I've learned that:

Some amends can't be made directly, but I can live differently today.

I may have to make amends more than once—especially when ego or poor timing got in the way.

God's timing is crucial; forcing amends too soon can cause more harm.

The real freedom of Step 8 is not dependent on someone else's response. It comes when I do my part and let God handle the rest.

Step 8 has taught me patience, humility, and the value of perseverance. Over the years, I've come to see Step 8 not as a one-time task, but as a continuing way of life.

When new situations arise where I've harmed someone, I don't wait. I add them to my list and become willing to make it right. Step 8 has become a daily practice of accountability, honesty, and humility.

The freedom I've found in this step is not about being perfect. It's about being willing—willing to face the truth, willing to take responsibility, and willing to trust God with the outcome.

Closing Prayer

"Lord, give me the courage to face the harm I have caused. Help me to see clearly the ripple effects of my sin and to take responsibility for my part. Make me willing to make amends to all those I have harmed, and guide me in Your timing and Your way. Where direct amends are not possible, help me to live in a way that honors You and demonstrates the change You have made in me. I trust You with the outcome. Amen."

STEP 9

We made direct amends to such people wherever possible, except when to do so would injure them or others.

Scripture Foundation

"If it is possible, as far as it depends on you, live at peace with everyone." (Romans 12:18) (NIV)

"Therefore, if you are offering your gift at the altar and there remember that your brother or sister has something against you, leave your gift there in front of the altar. First go and be reconciled to them; then come and offer your gift." (Matthew 5:23–24) (NIV)

"Bear with each other and forgive one another if any of you has a grievance against someone. Forgive as the Lord forgave you." (Colossians 3:13) (NIV)

Introduction – The Courage of Amends

Step 9 is where willingness becomes action. After prayerfully preparing in Step 8, we now take responsibility and begin making amends.

But Step 9 is not about demanding forgiveness or clearing our conscience at someone else's expense. It is about humility, courage, and discernment. Some amends can be made directly, face-to-face. Others may require indirect approaches, or may need to wait until God opens the door.

Step 9 is where preparation becomes reality. After praying, seeking counsel, and making our list in Step 8, we now take action by making direct amends—but with wisdom, humility, and prayerful timing.

Amends are not about demanding forgiveness or clearing our conscience at someone else's expense. They are about taking responsibility, cleaning up our side of the street, and seeking to restore peace where possible.

This step requires wisdom, prayer, and guidance from mentors. It also requires humility to accept that we cannot control how others respond. Our job is obedience—God handles the results.

There are times when direct amends may cause more harm than good. That's why this step requires discernment, counsel from mentors, and a willingness to trust God's timing.

Teaching & Lesson Content

Key Principles of Step 9

1. Direct Amends

Direct amends are face-to-face, spoken with humility and sincerity. This is the ideal form of amends when possible and appropriate. We approach the person we've harmed, take full responsibility for our actions, and express genuine remorse.

A direct amend includes:

- **Acknowledgment:** "I was wrong. Here's what I did."
- **Responsibility:** "This was my fault. I take full responsibility."
- **Apology:** "I am sorry for the harm I caused you."
- **Restitution (when possible):** "Here's what I'm doing to make it right."
- **Changed behavior:** "I'm committed to living differently."

Direct amends are not:

- Excuses or justifications.
- Explanations that shift blame.
- Demands for forgiveness.
- Opportunities to point out what the other person did wrong.

2. Indirect Amends

When direct contact would cause harm, find another way. Indirect amends include:

- **Letters never sent:** Writing out the amend for your own healing but not sending it if it would harm the recipient.
- **Prayer:** Praying for the person's healing and blessing.

- **Living amends:** Demonstrating change through consistent behavior over time.
- **Anonymous restitution:** Repaying a debt or making things right without direct contact.

Indirect amends are appropriate when:

- The person has passed away.
- The person has made it clear they don't want contact.
- Direct contact would reopen deep wounds.
- The amend would reveal information that would devastate the person or others.

3. No Expectations

We cannot control how others respond—only our obedience. The success of amends is measured by our obedience, not their reaction.

Some people will forgive us immediately. Others will need time. Some may never forgive us. That's not our responsibility. Our responsibility is to make the amend with humility and sincerity, and then release the outcome to God.

Step 9 is about freeing ourselves from guilt and shame by doing the right thing, regardless of how it's received.

4. Avoiding Harm

Do not reopen wounds unnecessarily or reveal truths that would devastate others. This is the "except when to do so would injure them or others" clause.

Examples of when not to make direct amends:

- Confessing an affair to a spouse when they don't know and it would destroy the marriage.
- Revealing details of past crimes that would implicate others.
- Contacting someone who has a restraining order against you.
- Approaching someone who is in a fragile emotional or mental state.

In these cases, seek counsel from your mentor or sponsor. Pray for wisdom. Consider indirect amends or living amends instead.

5. Living Amends

Sometimes the most powerful amend is living a new life of honesty, sobriety, and service. Living amends means that our life becomes the apology. We demonstrate through consistent actions, over time, that we are not the same person who caused the harm.

Living amends are especially important with family members who have been hurt repeatedly. Words alone won't convince them. They need to see sustained change—months and years of integrity, honesty, and faithfulness.

Living amends include:

- Staying sober and committed to recovery.
- Being honest in all our dealings.
- Showing up consistently for family and responsibilities.
- Serving others and giving back.
- Living in a way that honors God and reflects His transformation.

Story Box – My Personal Journey

When I began making amends, I quickly learned this step is not predictable. Some people welcomed me with forgiveness and grace. Others wanted nothing to do with me.

One family, still grieving the loss of their son to addiction, told me to get out of their face and never return. That rejection stung, but I had to remember: Step 9 isn't about how they respond. It's about me doing my part to make things right.

Financial amends were a long, grinding process. I spent over 10 years paying off debts to make things right. But each payment was an act of humility and perseverance. It taught me patience and the value of keeping my word, even when it was difficult.

Family amends were the hardest—not because of words, but because they were watching to see if my actions matched my promises. They tested me to see if I was truly changed. They had heard my apologies before, and they had seen me fail before. This time, they needed to see sustained change. That's when I learned that living amends often speak louder than words.

I also learned the importance of timing. Trying too soon sometimes caused more harm. There were amends I wanted to make immediately, but my sponsor advised me to wait. When I listened and trusted God's timing, doors opened that I could not have forced on my own. God showed me that living a life of ongoing amends—staying humble, faithful, and honest each day—is just as important as the words I spoke.

Some amends were welcomed with grace and forgiveness. Others were rejected outright. But whether the person forgave me or not, I had to release it to God. Step 9 is not about how people respond. It's about doing my part to make things right and leaving the results to God.

How to Make Amends

Before You Make the Amend

1. **Pray.** Ask God to prepare both your heart and the other person's heart.
2. **Seek counsel.** Talk to your mentor or sponsor about how to approach the amend.
3. **Plan what you'll say.** Write it out if necessary. Keep it simple, humble, and focused on your part.
4. **Check your motives.** Are you doing this to free yourself from guilt, or to genuinely make things right?

During the Amend

1. **Be humble.** Approach with a servant's heart, not with pride or defensiveness.
2. **Use "I" statements.** Focus only on your part. Don't bring up what they did.
3. **Take full responsibility.** No excuses, no justifications, no blame-shifting.
4. **Be specific.** Name what you did and how it affected them.
5. **Offer restitution if possible.** If you owe money, make a plan to pay it back. If you damaged property, offer to repair or replace it.
6. **Don't demand forgiveness.** Let them respond in their own time and way.

After the Amend

1. **Accept the outcome.** Whether they forgive you or not, release it to God.
2. **Don't defend yourself.** If they express anger or hurt, listen without arguing.
3. **Follow through.** If you promised to make financial restitution or change your behavior, keep your word.
4. **Practice living amends.** Show through your actions that you are different.

Examples of Amends

Financial Amend:

"I borrowed $500 from you three years ago and never paid it back. That was wrong, and I take full responsibility. I'm committed to making this right. Here's $100 today, and I'll pay you $50 a month until it's paid off."

Family Amend:

"I was absent and unreliable when you needed me most. I put my addiction above our relationship, and I caused you pain. I'm sorry. I can't undo the past, but I'm committed to being present and trustworthy from now on."

Workplace Amend:

"I lied about being sick when I was actually hungover. That was dishonest and unfair to you and the team. I take full responsibility. I'm committed to being honest and reliable moving forward."

Amend to a Child:

"I wasn't the parent you deserved. I was selfish and absent, and I hurt you. I'm so sorry. I can't change the past, but I'm working hard to be the parent you need today. I love you, and I'm committed to showing up for you."

Reflection Questions

Who on my Step 8 list is God prompting me to approach now?

_____

_____

_____

Am I willing to make an amend even if the other person rejects me?

_____

_____

_____

Am I prepared to practice living amends when direct ones aren't possible?

_____

_____

_____

How do I keep pride and ego out of the process of making amends?

_____

_____

_____

What fears do I feel about making these amends?

_____

_____

_____

Am I prepared for the possibility that they may reject me or not forgive me?

_____

_____

_____

Are there any amends I should wait on, to avoid harming someone further?

_____

_____

_____

What does "living amends" look like for me right now?

_____

_____

_____

Practical Application

- **Pray First:** Ask God to prepare both your heart and the other person's.
- **Plan Wisely:** Seek advice from your mentor or sponsor before making each amend.
- **Speak Humbly:** Use "I" statements, take full responsibility, and avoid excuses or blame.
- **Accept the Outcome:** Whether the person forgives you or not, release it to God.
- **Commit to Living Amends:** Prove your change through consistent sobriety and integrity.
- **Follow Through:** If you promised restitution, keep your word. If you said you'd change, demonstrate it through action.

Choice Point – Step 9

I can continue to hide from my past, or I can take responsibility and make things right.

- Will I have the courage to face those I've harmed, or will I avoid them?
- Will I make excuses, or will I take full responsibility?
- Will I demand forgiveness, or will I humbly offer an amend and release the outcome to God?

Today, I choose courage. I choose humility. I choose to make amends wherever possible and to trust God with the results.

Long-Term Reflection – Step 9

With time, I've come to see Step 9 as more than a checklist. It is a lifestyle of humility, honesty, and reconciliation.

I've learned that:

Some amends will never be accepted, but I can still live free from guilt.

Not all wounds heal quickly, but I can live free from guilt when I've done my part.

Some people may never forgive me, but I can forgive myself and keep walking in freedom.

Living amends often speak louder than words—especially with family.

God's timing matters—and patience is often part of the healing.

True freedom comes when I release the results to God and walk in obedience.

This step requires constant humility and reliance on God's wisdom.

Step 9 taught me that while I cannot undo the past, I can live in such a way today that my very life becomes an amend—a testimony of God's grace and power to transform.

Step 9 has taught me that while I can't undo the past, I can live in such a way today that my life itself becomes an amend—a testimony of God's grace at work in me.

Amends don't end once I've crossed off a list—they continue as I live differently today. Every day is an opportunity to demonstrate through my actions that I am not the same person I once was. Every day is a living amend.

Closing Prayer

"Lord, give me the courage to make amends to those I have harmed. Help me to approach each person with humility and sincerity, taking full responsibility for my actions. Prepare their hearts to receive my amend, but help me to release the outcome to You. Where direct amends would cause harm, show me how to make living amends through my changed life. Thank You for Your grace that makes restoration possible. Amen."

STEP 10

We continued to take personal inventory, and when we were wrong, promptly admitted it.

Scripture Foundation

"So, if you think you are standing firm, be careful that you don't fall!" (1 Corinthians 10:12) (NIV)

"Search me, God, and know my heart; test me and know my anxious thoughts. See if there is any offensive way in me, and lead me in the way everlasting." (Psalm 139:23–24) (NIV)

"Therefore confess your sins to each other and pray for each other so that you may be healed." (James 5:16) (NIV)

Introduction – Daily Honesty for Daily Freedom

Step 10 is about living in the present. After cleaning house in Steps 4–9, we now commit to keeping it clean. Instead of letting new resentments, fears, or selfish actions pile up, we take daily inventory.

This step is about daily maintenance. We don't wait until problems pile up; we take daily inventory, recognizing when pride, fear, or selfishness creep back in. When we're wrong, we admit it promptly— before it grows into new resentments.

This step prevents relapse by teaching us to deal with issues immediately. It's not about perfection, but about progress and honesty. When we are wrong, we admit it quickly and make it right—before shame and guilt can grow again.

Step 10 keeps us humble, accountable, and free. It's a safeguard against relapse into old thinking and behaviors. It's the difference between staying in recovery and sliding back into old patterns.

Teaching & Lesson Content

1. Ongoing Inventory

Step 4 was the big inventory—the thorough, searching look at our entire past. Step 10 is the daily one—the regular check-in that keeps us honest and humble.

Think of Step 4 as the deep cleaning of a house, and Step 10 as the daily tidying up. We don't wait for the mess to pile up again. We deal with it as it comes, one day at a time.

Daily inventory means we regularly pause to examine:

- Our thoughts and attitudes.
- Our words and actions.
- Our motives and intentions.
- Our relationships and responsibilities.

We ask ourselves: Where did I do well today? Where did I fall short? Did I harm anyone? Do I owe anyone an apology?

2. Prompt Admission

The key is to admit wrongs quickly, before they gain power. The longer we wait to admit a mistake, the more shame and guilt build up. The more shame and guilt build up, the harder it becomes to admit the wrong.

Step 10 breaks this cycle by teaching us to deal with issues immediately. When we recognize we've been wrong—whether in thought, word, or deed—we admit it right away. We don't wait. We don't justify. We don't minimize. We simply say, "I was wrong. I'm sorry."

Prompt admission keeps us free. It prevents small wrongs from becoming big resentments. It keeps our relationships healthy. It keeps our conscience clear.

3. Prevention vs. Repair

Step 10 prevents new harm from becoming new wreckage. It's much easier to deal with a small issue today than to let it grow into a major problem tomorrow.

When we practice daily inventory and prompt admission, we catch problems early. We address resentments before they take root. We apologize for harsh words before they damage relationships. We correct dishonesty before it becomes a pattern.

Prevention is always easier than repair. Step 10 is our daily prevention plan.

4. Humility in Action

Staying teachable and correctable keeps us growing. Step 10 requires humility—the willingness to admit when we're wrong, to accept correction, and to keep learning.

Pride says, "I don't need to admit that. It wasn't that bad." Humility says, "I was wrong, and I need to make it right."

Pride says, "They should apologize first." Humility says, "I'll clean up my side of the street, regardless of what they do."

Pride says, "I've already worked the steps. I don't need to keep doing this." Humility says, "I need daily maintenance to stay free."

Step 10 is humility in action. It's the daily choice to stay honest, stay accountable, and stay free.

5. Living in the Present

Step 10 keeps us focused on today. We're not dwelling on the past (that's been dealt with in Steps 4–9). We're not worrying about the future (that's in God's hands). We're living in the present, dealing with today's issues today.

This is the essence of "one day at a time." We take inventory today. We admit wrongs today. We make amends today. We stay free today.

Story Box – My Personal Journey

When I first came into recovery, I thought my big Step 4 and Step 5 were enough. But I quickly learned that new mistakes happen daily. If I didn't deal with them immediately, they piled up and pulled me backward.

Step 10 became a lifestyle for me. Whether it was snapping at someone, being prideful, or failing to follow through on my word—I learned to stop, admit it, and make it right. The more quickly I admitted wrong, the more peace I had.

I learned quickly that if I don't practice Step 10, my old patterns creep back in. Pride, selfishness, and anger don't disappear overnight. Daily inventory has helped me see when I'm starting to slip and correct it before it damages relationships. This step has taught me to stay honest, humble, and teachable.

There have been countless times when Step 10 saved me from sliding back into resentment or relapse. A harsh word spoken in anger, a moment of dishonesty, a flash of pride—if I had let these things sit, they would have grown. But because I dealt with them immediately, they lost their power.

Step 10 is not about being perfect. It's about being honest and humble enough to admit wrongs quickly. It's about staying free, one day at a time.

Daily Inventory Guide

1. Morning Check-In

Start each day with a brief inventory and prayer:

Questions to ask:

- What attitudes or fears am I carrying into today?
- What choices do I need God's help with?
- Are there any unresolved issues from yesterday that I need to address?
- What challenges might I face today, and how can I prepare?

Morning Prayer:

"Lord, order my steps today. Keep me humble and honest. Help me to walk in Your ways and to admit quickly when I'm wrong. Guide my thoughts, words, and actions. Amen."

2. Evening Review

End each day with a thorough review:

Questions to ask:

- Where did I do well today?
- Where did I fall short?
- Did I harm anyone with my words or actions?
- Do I owe someone an apology or restitution?
- Where did I see pride, fear, selfishness, or dishonesty show up?
- How did I respond to challenges or conflicts?
- Did I practice the principles of recovery today?

Evening Prayer:

"Lord, search my heart. Show me where I missed the mark today. Give me the courage to make it right tomorrow. Thank You for Your grace and mercy. Amen."

3. Spot-Check Inventory

Throughout the day, pause when you feel disturbed or upset:

Questions to ask:

- What just happened?
- How did I respond?
- Was I wrong in my reaction?
- Do I need to make an immediate amend?
- What defect is showing up right now (pride, fear, anger, selfishness)?

Immediate Action:

If you recognize you were wrong, admit it right away. Don't wait until the end of the day. Deal with it in the moment.

4. Prompt Admission

Don't wait. If you recognize a wrong, admit it immediately.

Examples:

- "I was wrong when I spoke harshly to you earlier. Please forgive me."
- "I exaggerated that story to make myself look better. That was dishonest, and I'm sorry."
- "I was impatient and short with you. That wasn't fair. I apologize."

Examples of Step 10 in Action

Example 1:

"Today, I noticed I exaggerated a story to look better. I admitted it to the group and corrected it. I felt embarrassed, but I also felt free."

Example 2:

"I was impatient with my coworker. Instead of ignoring it, I apologized the same day. It kept the relationship healthy and my conscience clear."

Example 3:

"I felt resentment toward a family member. I wrote it down and prayed for God to remove it before it grew. By the next day, the resentment was gone."

Example 4:

"I snapped at my spouse this morning. I immediately recognized it was wrong and apologized. We talked it through, and it didn't turn into a bigger conflict."

Example 5:

"I caught myself gossiping about someone. I stopped mid-sentence, admitted I was wrong, and changed the subject. It felt uncomfortable, but it was the right thing to do."

Reflection Questions

Do I regularly take time to review my day?

_____

How quickly do I admit when I am wrong?

_____

Am I more concerned with being right, or with staying free?

_____

Where do I see pride or fear keeping me from honest admission?

_____

Do I pause daily to reflect on my thoughts, actions, and attitudes?

_____

Am I quick to admit when I'm wrong, or do I still delay and justify?

_____

How do I practice daily honesty with God, myself, and others?

_____

What patterns do I notice in my daily inventory? Are there recurring defects I need to address?

_____

Practical Application

- **Start a daily journal:** Write down 3 victories and 3 areas needing growth each day.
- **Share one area of failure** with a mentor or accountability partner each week.
- **Before bed, pray Psalm 139:23–24,** asking God to reveal any hidden faults.
- **Daily Review:** At night, ask: "Where was I selfish, dishonest, resentful, or fearful today?"
- **Quick Amends:** If you wrong someone, apologize immediately. Don't let it sit.
- **Accountability Partner:** Share your daily inventory with a mentor or peer regularly.
- **Morning and Evening Prayers:** Use the prayers above to bookend your day with honesty and humility.

Choice Point – Step 10

I can either cover my wrongs and let them grow, or I can admit them and stay free.

- Will I ignore my faults, or will I deal with them quickly?
- Will I protect my pride, or will I choose humility?
- Will I let resentments and guilt pile up, or will I address them daily?

Today, I choose honesty—to admit my wrongs and walk in freedom. I choose humility over pride, and prompt admission over delayed justification.

Long-Term Reflection – Step 10

Over the years, Step 10 has kept me free. It's not about being flawless—it's about being honest and humble enough to admit wrongs quickly.

This step has saved me countless times from sliding back into resentment or relapse. Step 10 reminds me that recovery is not a one-time event, but a daily walk of honesty, humility, and grace.

Step 10 is not about perfection, but about progress. The longer I walk this out, the quicker I recognize defects when they show up—and the quicker I can surrender them to God. This daily maintenance keeps me from carrying new guilt and helps me stay free.

I've learned that the more consistently I practice Step 10, the easier it becomes. Daily inventory becomes a natural part of my routine. Prompt admission becomes second nature. Humility becomes a way of life.

I've also learned that Step 10 protects my relationships. When I deal with issues immediately, conflicts don't escalate. Misunderstandings don't turn into resentments. Small mistakes don't become big problems.

Most importantly, Step 10 keeps me close to God. Daily inventory keeps me aware of my need for Him. Prompt admission keeps me humble. And living in the present keeps me grateful for His grace, one day at a time.

Step 10 is the step that keeps all the other steps alive. It's the daily practice that sustains long-term recovery. It's the difference between staying free and falling back into bondage.

Closing Prayer

"Lord, help me to practice daily honesty. Give me the courage to take inventory each day and to admit promptly when I am wrong. Keep me humble, teachable, and accountable. Protect me from pride, resentment, and fear. Help me to live in the present, dealing with today's issues today, and trusting You with tomorrow. Thank You for Your daily grace. Amen."

STEP 11

We sought through prayer and meditation to improve our conscious contact with God, praying only for knowledge of His will for us and the power to carry that out.

Scripture Foundation

"Be still, and know that I am God." (Psalm 46:10) (NIV)

"Your word is a lamp to my feet and a light to my path." (Psalm 119:105) (NIV)

"Pray continually, give thanks in all circumstances; for this is God's will for you in Christ Jesus." (1 Thessalonians 5:17–18) (NIV)

"Do not conform to the pattern of this world, but be transformed by the renewing of your mind. Then you will be able to test and approve what God's will is—his good, pleasing and perfect will." (Romans 12:2) (NIV)

Introduction – Growing in Relationship

Step 11 is about connection. Sobriety without spiritual growth leaves us empty. Prayer and meditation are not religious rituals—they are daily practices of intimacy with God.

This step is not about getting God to do what we want but about aligning our will with His. As we pray and meditate, we grow in awareness of His presence, learn to hear His voice, and receive strength to do His will.

Step 11 is the heart of spiritual growth. It's not just about avoiding relapse—it's about deepening our relationship with God. Through prayer, Scripture, and meditation, we learn to hear His voice, trust His guidance, and obey His will.

This step reminds us that recovery is not self-improvement—it's about staying connected to the Source of life. Without this connection, we drift. With it, we thrive.

Teaching & Lesson Content

1. Conscious Contact

Conscious contact means more than believing in God—it's about daily awareness of His presence. It's living with the knowledge that God is with us, guiding us, speaking to us, and empowering us.

Many of us have believed in God for years, but we've never developed a real relationship with Him. We've prayed when we were in trouble, but we haven't learned to walk with Him daily. Step 11 calls us to move beyond casual belief into an intimate relationship.

Conscious contact means:

- Being aware of God's presence throughout the day.
- Listening for His voice in Scripture, prayer, and circumstances.
- Seeking His will in decisions, relationships, and daily choices.
- Depending on His power to live out what He calls us to do.

This is not a one-time experience. It's a daily, ongoing relationship that grows deeper over time.

2. Prayer – Talking Honestly with God

Prayer is talking honestly with God about our needs, struggles, and gratitude. It's not about using fancy words or following a formula. It's about being real with God.

In Step 11, we learn to pray differently than we may have prayed before. Instead of praying for what we want, we pray for knowledge of God's will and the power to carry it out.

Types of Prayer:

Confession: "Lord, I was wrong today. I acted in pride/fear/selfishness. Forgive me and change me."

Gratitude: "Thank You for Your faithfulness, for my sobriety, for the people You've placed in my life."

Petition: "Lord, I need Your help with [situation]. Show me Your will and give me strength to follow it."

Intercession: "I pray for [person]. Bless them, heal them, guide them."

Surrender: "Not my will, but Yours be done. I trust You with this situation."

3. Meditation – Listening in Stillness

Meditation is listening in stillness, reflecting on His Word, and letting it shape us. While prayer is talking to God, meditation is listening to God.

In our culture, we're constantly bombarded with noise—media, notifications, demands, distractions. Meditation requires us to slow down, be still, and create space to hear God's voice.

Biblical meditation is different from Eastern meditation.

We're not emptying our minds; we're filling them with God's truth. We're not seeking a blank state; we're seeking God's presence.

How to Meditate on Scripture:

1. **Read** a passage slowly and carefully.
2. **Reflect** on what it says. What does this teach me about God? About myself? About how I should live?
3. **Pray** the passage back to God. Ask Him to apply it to your life.
4. **Listen** in silence. Sit quietly and let God's Spirit speak to your heart.
5. **Obey** what God reveals. Meditation without obedience is just information.

4. Knowledge of His Will and Power to Carry It Out

Step 11 reminds us to pray for two things: knowledge of God's will and the power to carry it out.

Knowledge of His will: We seek to know what God wants for us—not what we want from Him. We ask: "Lord, what do You want me to do? How do You want me to live? What is Your plan for my life?"

Power to carry it out: Knowing God's will is not enough. We also need His power to obey it. We pray: "Lord, give me the strength, courage, and wisdom to do what You're calling me to do."

This keeps us humble and dependent on God. We're not trying to live the Christian life in our own strength. We're relying on His power working in us.

5. Recovery Is Really About Relationship

The longer we walk with God, the more we see that His will is always better than ours. Step 11 shows us that recovery is not just about staying sober—it's about staying connected to God.

When we neglect prayer and meditation, we drift. When we stop listening, we stumble. But when we seek God daily, our recovery deepens and our purpose grows clearer.

Step 11 reminds us that lasting sobriety is built not on willpower, but on a relationship with Christ.

Story Box – My Personal Journey

Prayer and meditation became lifelines for me. Early on, I prayed mostly for God to fix my problems. Over time, I learned prayer is not about bending God's will to mine, but about surrendering my will to His.

Meditation on Scripture opened my heart in new ways. Some mornings, a single verse carried me all day. The more I practiced, the more I realized Step 11 wasn't just about sobriety—it was about building a real relationship with Jesus.

Early in recovery, I prayed mostly for what I wanted. Over time, I've learned to ask instead: "God, what do You want for me today?" This change has deepened my faith and kept me steady in difficult seasons.

Step 11 has shown me that recovery without prayer becomes fragile. Over the years, I've seen that when I stop praying, I drift. When I stop listening, I stumble. But when I seek God daily, my recovery deepens and my purpose grows clearer.

There have been times when I've gotten busy and let my prayer life slip. Every time, I've noticed the difference. My peace fades. My patience wears thin. My old thinking patterns creep back in. But when I return to daily prayer and meditation, I'm reminded that I cannot do this on my own. I need God every single day.

Step 11 has taught me that the quality of my relationship with God directly affects the quality of my recovery. The more time I spend with Him, the stronger I become. The more I listen to His voice, the clearer my path becomes.

Prayer & Meditation Guide

1. Daily Prayer Routine

Morning Prayer:

"Lord, guide my thoughts, words, and actions today. Show me Your will and give me the power to carry it out. Keep me humble, honest, and dependent on You. Order my steps and help me to walk in Your ways. Amen."

Midday Check-In:

Pause during the day and ask: "Am I walking in Your will right now? Is there anything I need to surrender or confess?"

Evening Prayer:

"Thank You, Lord, for today. Show me where I fell short, and strengthen me for tomorrow. I surrender this day to You and trust You with what's ahead. Amen."

2. Scripture Meditation

Step-by-Step Process:

1. **Read** a short passage (Psalms, Proverbs, Gospels, or other Scripture).
2. **Reflect:** What does this teach me about God? About myself? About how I should live?
3. **Pray:** Ask God to apply it to your life. "Lord, how does this truth apply to me today?"
4. **Listen:** Sit in silence for a few minutes, letting God's Spirit speak to your heart.
5. **Obey:** Take action on what God reveals.

Suggested Passages for Meditation:

- Psalm 23 (God as Shepherd)
- Psalm 51 (Confession and renewal)
- Proverbs 3:5–6 (Trust and surrender)

- Matthew 6:25–34 (Worry and trust)
- Romans 12:1–2 (Living sacrifice and transformation)
- Philippians 4:6–7 (Peace through prayer)

3. Journaling

What to Journal:

- Prayers (write them out)
- Gratitude lists (what you're thankful for)
- Verses that stand out (and what they mean to you)
- Answered prayers (to build faith over time)
- What God is teaching you
- Areas where you need to grow

Journaling helps us process our thoughts, track our spiritual growth, and remember God's faithfulness.

4. Listening Posture

Practice silence and openness in prayer. After you've prayed, sit quietly and listen. Don't rush. Don't fill the silence with more words. Just be still and let God speak.

God's voice is often quiet and gentle. It comes through Scripture, through the prompting of the Holy Spirit, through wise counsel, through circumstances. The more we practice listening, the better we become at recognizing His voice.

Examples of Step 11 in Action

Example 1:

"I prayed Psalm 23 each morning for a week, and it reminded me daily that God is my shepherd. I felt His peace and guidance throughout each day."

Example 2:

"During meditation, I realized I was holding resentment toward a coworker. God showed me to forgive. I prayed for them and released the resentment."

Example 3:

"By journaling answered prayers, I saw how faithful God had been over months. It strengthened my faith and reminded me that He is always working, even when I can't see it."

Example 4:

"I was anxious about a decision. I spent time in prayer and meditation, asking God for His will. By the end of the week, I had clarity and peace about what to do."

Example 5:

"I started each day with 10 minutes of silence and Scripture. It transformed my mornings and set the tone for the entire day."

Reflection Questions

Do I set aside regular time to pray and listen to God?

_____

How do I know when I am seeking His will versus my own?

_____

What Scriptures help me stay grounded in recovery?

_____

Where do I need more discipline in prayer or meditation?

_____

Do I set aside daily time to connect with God?

_____

Am I seeking God's will, or still asking Him to bless my own plans?

_____

How do I listen for God's voice beyond my own thoughts?

_____

What distractions keep me from spending time with God?

_____

How has my relationship with God grown since I began recovery?

_____

Practical Application

- **Commit to 10 minutes of daily prayer and meditation this week.** Start small and build consistency.
- **Choose one Scripture each day to meditate on and carry with you.** Write it on a card or set it as a reminder on your phone.
- **Write out a prayer asking God to reveal His will for one area of your life.** Be specific and honest.
- **Prayer Routine:** Begin and end the day in prayer. Make it a non-negotiable part of your routine.
- **Meditation:** Reflect on Scripture and ask God how it applies to your life today.
- **Listening Posture:** Practice silence and openness in prayer. Don't rush. Be still.
- **Journal your prayers and answered prayers.** Track God's faithfulness over time.

Choice Point – Step 11

- I can either live by my own will, or I can seek God's will through prayer and meditation.

- Will I rush through life without listening, or will I slow down to hear God's voice?
- Will I keep demanding my way, or will I seek His way?
- Will I rely on my own strength, or will I depend on His power?

Today, I choose connection—to grow in conscious contact with God. I choose to seek His will and trust His power to carry it out.

Long-Term Reflection – Step 11

Step 11 has shown me that recovery without prayer becomes fragile. Over the years, I've seen that when I stop praying, I drift. When I stop listening, I stumble.

But when I seek God daily, my recovery deepens and my purpose grows clearer. Step 11 reminds me that lasting sobriety is built not on willpower, but on a relationship with Christ.

The longer I walk with God, the more I see that His will is always better than mine. This daily practice keeps me anchored and gives me the strength to face whatever comes.

I've learned that Step 11 is not just a step—it's a way of life. It's the foundation of everything else. When my relationship with God is strong, everything else falls into place. When I neglect it, everything else suffers.

Step 11 has taught me that recovery is really about relationship. The closer I draw to God, the freer I become. The more I seek His will, the more peace I experience. The more I depend on His power, the stronger I grow.

This is the step that sustains all the others. This is the step that keeps me free.

Closing Prayer

"Lord, I seek to know You more deeply each day. Teach me to pray, to listen, and to obey. Help me to grow in conscious contact with You through prayer and meditation. Show me Your will for my life and give me the power to carry it out. I surrender my plans, my desires, and my will to You. Not my will, but Yours be done. Thank You for Your presence, Your guidance, and Your power. Amen."

STEP 12

Having had a spiritual awakening as the result of these steps, we tried to carry this message to others, and to practice these principles in all our affairs.

Scripture Foundation

"They triumphed over him by the blood of the Lamb and by the word of their testimony; they did not love their lives so much as to shrink from death." (Revelation 12:11) (NIV)

"Freely you have received; freely give." (Matthew 10:8) (NIV)

"Therefore go and make disciples of all nations, baptizing them in the name of the Father and of the Son and of the Holy Spirit, and teaching them to obey everything I have commanded you. And surely I am with you always, to the very end of the age." (Matthew 28:19–20) (NIV)

"You are the light of the world. A town built on a hill cannot be hidden. Neither do people light a lamp and put it under a bowl. Instead they put it on its stand, and it gives light to everyone in the house. In the same way, let your light shine before others, that they may see your good deeds and glorify your Father in heaven." (Matthew 5:14–16) (NIV)

Introduction – The Fruit and the Mission

Step 12 is both the fruit and the mission of recovery. Having experienced transformation, we are now called to give it away—to carry the message of hope to others still trapped in addiction, and to live out these principles in every area of our lives.

This step is where recovery becomes discipleship and service. We are not saved just for ourselves—we are saved to serve. The freedom we've received is not meant to be hoarded; it's meant to be shared.

Step 12 has three parts:

1. **Spiritual awakening** – recognizing the transformation God has worked in us.
2. **Carrying the message** – sharing our story and helping others find freedom.

3. **Practicing these principles** – living out recovery in every area of life.

This is the step that gives our recovery purpose. This is the step that turns our pain into ministry and our testimony into hope for others.

Teaching & Lesson Content

1. Spiritual Awakening

A spiritual awakening is the recognition that God has done something profound in our lives. We are not who we used to be. The old has gone, the new has come (2 Corinthians 5:17).

For some, this awakening is dramatic—a moment of radical transformation like Paul on the road to Damascus. For others, it's gradual—a slow, steady change that becomes undeniable over time.

Either way, spiritual awakening means:

- We see ourselves differently (no longer defined by our addiction).
- We see God differently (knowing Him personally, not just knowing about Him).
- We see others differently (with compassion instead of judgment).
- We see life differently (with purpose, hope, and gratitude).

This awakening is not something we manufacture. It's the result of working the steps, surrendering to God, and allowing Him to transform us from the inside out.

2. Carrying the Message

Once we've experienced freedom, we're called to share it. Carrying the message means telling our story—not to brag about how far we've come, but to point others to the God who saved us.

Our testimony has power. Revelation 12:11 says we overcome by the blood of the Lamb and the word of our testimony. When we share what God has done in our lives, it encourages others, breaks the power of shame, and points people to Jesus.

Carrying the message includes:

- **Sharing your story** – being honest about where you've been and what God has done.
- **Sponsoring or mentoring** – walking alongside someone new in recovery.
- **Serving in recovery groups** – volunteering, leading meetings, offering support.
- **Being available** – answering calls, offering encouragement, showing up when someone needs help.
- **Living authentically** – being a living example of God's grace and transformation.

We don't carry the message because we're perfect. We carry it because we're grateful. We carry it because someone carried it to us when we needed it most.

3. Practicing These Principles in All Our Affairs

Recovery is not just for meetings. It's for every area of life—home, work, relationships, finances, church, community.

Practicing these principles means:

- **Honesty** – in all our dealings, not just in recovery circles.
- **Humility** – admitting when we're wrong, staying teachable.
- **Surrender** – trusting God's will in every decision.
- **Accountability** – staying connected to mentors, sponsors, and community.
- **Service** – looking for ways to help others, not just ourselves.
- **Gratitude** – living with thankfulness for what God has done.
- **Daily inventory** – continuing to examine our hearts and make things right.
- **Prayer and meditation** – staying connected to God every day.

Step 12 calls us to live out our recovery 24/7. It's not something we turn on and off. It's a way of life.

4. Recovery Becomes Discipleship

Step 12 is where recovery and discipleship merge. We realize that the 12 steps are not just about getting sober—they're about becoming disciples of Jesus Christ.

Jesus calls us to:

- Deny ourselves (Step 1–3)
- Take up our cross daily (Step 10)
- Follow Him (Step 11)
- Make disciples (Step 12)

Recovery is discipleship. Discipleship is recovery. Both require surrender, transformation, and a life of service.

5. We Are Saved to Serve

God didn't rescue us just so we could live comfortable, self-focused lives. He rescued us so we could be His hands and feet in a broken world.

Our addiction once made us takers—we used people, manipulated situations, and lived for ourselves. But recovery transforms us into givers—we serve, encourage, and point others to Jesus.

Step 12 reminds us that our lives are not our own. We've been bought with a price (1 Corinthians 6:19–20). We've been set free for a purpose. And that purpose is to carry the message of hope to others who are still in bondage.

Story Box – My Personal Journey

For me, Step 12 has become a calling. God didn't just save me from addiction—He called me to share my story and help others find freedom. Every time I share my testimony, I'm reminded of God's grace and renewed in my own recovery.

I've learned that carrying the message is not a burden—it's a privilege. When I see someone's eyes light up with hope, when I watch someone take their first steps toward freedom, when I hear someone say, "If God can change you, maybe He can change me too"—that's when I know my pain had a purpose.

The more I live Step 12, the more I see that recovery isn't about what I've lost, but about what I've gained—a purpose bigger than myself. Serving others not only strengthens my recovery, it fulfills my calling in Christ to be a light in the darkness.

I've also learned that I can't give away what I don't have. If I'm not working my own program, if I'm not staying connected to God, if I'm not practicing these principles in my own life, I have nothing to offer. Step 12 requires me to stay healthy, stay humble, and stay dependent on God.

But when I do, when I stay connected to the Source, God uses my story in ways I never imagined. He takes my mess and turns it into a message. He takes my pain and turns it into purpose. And that's the beauty of Step 12.

The Three Parts of Step 12

Part 1: Having Had a Spiritual Awakening

Reflection Questions:

How has God changed me since I began recovery?

_____

_____

_____

What areas of my life look different now than they did before?

_____

_____

_____

How would I describe my spiritual awakening to someone else?

_____

_____

_____

Am I still experiencing growth, or have I become complacent?

_____

_____

_____

Practical Application:

- Write out your testimony. Include where you were, what God did, and where you are now.
- Share your testimony with someone this week—in a meeting, with a friend, or with someone who needs hope.

Part 2: We Tried to Carry This Message to Others

Reflection Questions:

Who in my life needs to hear my testimony of God's grace?

_____

_____

_____

How can I serve others in recovery today?

_____

_____

_____

Am I willing to mentor or sponsor someone new in recovery?

_____

_____

_____

What opportunities has God given me to share my story?

_____

_____

_____

Practical Application:

- **Service:** Volunteer in recovery groups, church, or community outreach.
- **Sponsorship:** Mentor someone new in recovery. Walk with them through the steps.

- **Availability:** Make yourself available to answer calls, offer encouragement, and show up when someone needs help.
- **Testimony:** Share your story in meetings, at church, or in conversations with those who are struggling.

Part 3: Practice These Principles in All Our Affairs

Reflection Questions:

Am I practicing these principles not just in meetings, but at home, at work, and in the community?

_____

_____

_____

Where do I struggle to live out recovery principles?

_____

_____

_____

How can I be more honest, humble, and accountable in my daily life?

_____

_____

_____

What areas of my life still need to be surrendered to God?

_____

_____

_____

Practical Application:

- **Lifestyle:** Let your daily choices reflect the freedom you've received.
- **Integrity:** Be honest in all your dealings—at work, at home, in relationships.
- **Humility:** Admit when you're wrong. Stay teachable. Accept correction.
- **Service:** Look for ways to serve others every day—not just in recovery, but everywhere.
- **Accountability:** Stay connected to your mentor, sponsor, and recovery community.

The Power of Testimony

Your story matters. Your testimony has power. When you share what God has done in your life, you:

- Give hope to those who feel hopeless.
- Break the power of shame and secrecy.
- Point people to Jesus, not to yourself.
- Strengthen your own recovery by remembering where you came from.
- Fulfill God's purpose for your life.

Don't wait until you're "perfect" to share your story. You don't have to have it all together. You just have to be honest about what God has done.

How to Share Your Testimony:

1. **Where you were** – Briefly describe your life before recovery (without glorifying the addiction).
2. **What God did** – Share the moment or process of transformation. How did God meet you? What changed?
3. **Where you are now** – Describe the freedom, hope, and purpose you've found in recovery.
4. **Point to Jesus** – Make sure your testimony points to God's grace, not your own strength.

Keep it simple, honest, and focused on God's work in your life.

Reflection Questions

Who in my life needs to hear my testimony of God's grace?

_____

_____

_____

How can I serve others in recovery today?

_____

_____

_____

Am I practicing these principles not just in meetings, but at home, at work, and in the community?

_____

_____

_____

How has God changed me since I began recovery?

_____

_____

_____

What areas of my life look different now than they did before?

_____

_____

_____

Am I willing to mentor or sponsor someone new in recovery?

_____

_____

_____

What opportunities has God given me to share my story?

_____

_____

_____

Where do I struggle to live out recovery principles?

_____

_____

_____

How can I be more honest, humble, and accountable in my daily life?

_____

_____

_____

Practical Application

- **Service:** Volunteer in recovery groups, church, or community outreach.
- **Sponsorship:** Mentor someone new in recovery. Walk with them through the steps.
- **Lifestyle:** Let your daily choices reflect the freedom you've received.
- **Testimony:** Write out your testimony and share it with someone this week.
- **Availability:** Make yourself available to answer calls, offer encouragement, and show up when someone needs help.
- **Integrity:** Be honest in all your dealings—at work, at home, in relationships.
- **Gratitude:** Thank God daily for your recovery and for the opportunity to serve others.

Choice Point – Step 12

I can keep my recovery to myself, or I can share it with others.

- Will I hoard the freedom I've received, or will I give it away?
- Will I live for myself, or will I live to serve others?
- Will I practice these principles only when it's convenient, or will I live them out in every area of my life?

Today, I choose to carry the message. I choose to serve. I choose to live out these principles in all my affairs. I choose to be a light in the darkness.

Long-Term Reflection – Step 12

The more I live Step 12, the more I see that recovery isn't about what I've lost, but about what I've gained—a purpose bigger than myself. Serving others not only strengthens my recovery, it fulfills my calling in Christ to be a light in the darkness.

I've learned that I can't keep what I have unless I give it away. The more I serve, the stronger my recovery becomes. The more I share my story, the more I remember God's faithfulness. The more I practice these principles, the more freedom I experience.

Step 12 has taught me that my life is not my own. I've been rescued for a reason. I've been set free for a purpose. And that purpose is to point others to the God who saved me.

This is not a burden—it's a privilege. This is not an obligation—it's a calling. This is not the end of the journey—it's the beginning of a life of purpose, service, and joy.

Step 12 is where recovery becomes a way of life. It's where our pain becomes our ministry. It's where our testimony becomes hope for others. And it's where we discover that the greatest joy in recovery is not what we receive, but what we give away.

Closing Prayer

"Lord, thank You for the spiritual awakening You have given me. Thank You for rescuing me from addiction and giving me a new life. Help me to carry this message to others who are still in bondage. Give me opportunities to share my story and to serve those who need hope. Help me to practice these principles in every area of my life—at home, at work, in my relationships, and in my community. Use my pain for Your purpose. Use my testimony for Your glory. I surrender my life to You, not just for my own freedom, but so that others may find freedom too. Amen."

Living a Christ-Centered Life

The 12 Steps lead us to freedom in Christ, but the journey does not end there. Recovery is not only about breaking free from the past—it is about living fully in the new life Christ provides. Part Three equips us to live as disciples of Jesus, walking in our new identity, discovering our purpose, pressing on with determination, bearing spiritual fruit, and persevering in long-term faith and service. These final chapters focus on sustaining a Christ-centered life that endures and multiplies.

Identity in Christ

In recovery, it is vital to know who we are in Christ. We are no longer defined by our past mistakes, but by God's grace. Our new identity is as sons and daughters of God, redeemed and chosen for His glory.

Key Scriptures:

• 2 Corinthians 5:17 (NIV)– *"If anyone is in Christ, the new creation has come: The old has gone, the new is here!"*

• Ephesians 1:4–5 (NIV) *"He chose us in Him before the creation of the world... In love He predestined us for adoption to sonship through Jesus Christ."*

Reflection Questions:

How does knowing your identity in Christ change how you see yourself?

_____

_____

_____

What lies from your past do you need to replace with God's truth?

_____

_____

_____

Prayer Focus:

Thank God for making you a new creation and ask Him to help you live confidently in your identity in Christ.

Discovering Purpose and Calling

God has created each of us with a unique purpose. Discovering that purpose gives meaning to our recovery. We are saved not only from sin, but for good works that God prepared in advance for us to do. Walking in our calling brings joy, fulfillment, and impact for God's kingdom.

Key Scriptures:

• Jeremiah 29:11 (NIV) – _"For I know the plans I have for you, declares the Lord… plans to give you hope and a future."_

• Ephesians 2:10 (NIV) – _"For we are God's handiwork, created in Christ Jesus to do good works, which God prepared in advance for us to do."_

Reflection Questions:

What gifts or passions has God placed in your heart that can be used for His glory?

_____

_____

_____

How might your recovery journey shape your calling to serve others?

_____

_____

_____

Prayer Focus:

Ask God to reveal His purpose for your life and to guide you in walking out your calling.

Determination & Pressing On

Living a Christ-centered life requires perseverance. We will face trials, temptations, and setbacks, but God gives us the strength to press on. Determination rooted in faith helps us endure and grow in maturity.

Key Scriptures:

• Philippians 3:13–14 (NIV) – *"Forgetting what is behind and straining toward what is ahead, I press on toward the goal to win the prize for which God has called me heavenward in Christ Jesus."*

• James 1:2–4 (NIV) – *"Consider it pure joy, my brothers and sisters, whenever you face trials of many kinds, because you know that the testing of your faith produces perseverance. Let perseverance finish its work so that you may be mature and complete, not lacking anything. "*

Reflection Questions:

What challenges are testing your determination right now?

_____

_____

_____

How can you keep pressing on toward Christ even in trials?

_____

_____

_____

Prayer Focus:

Pray for endurance and determination to continue pressing on in your walk with Christ.

The Fruit of the Spirit in Daily Life

As disciples of Christ, our lives should demonstrate the fruit of the Spirit. The Spirit transforms our character and produces love, joy, peace, patience, kindness, goodness, faithfulness, gentleness, and self-control. This fruit is evidence of Christ living in us.

Key Scriptures:

• Galatians 5:22–23 (NIV) – *"The fruit of the Spirit is love, joy, peace, forbearance, kindness, goodness, faithfulness, gentleness and self-control."*

• John 15:5 (NIV) – *"I am the vine; you are the branches. If you remain in me and I in you, you will bear much fruit; apart from me you can do nothing."*

Reflection Questions:

_____

_____

_____

Which fruit of the Spirit do you see most evident in your life?

_____

_____

_____

Which fruit do you want God to develop more fully in you?

_____

_____

_____

Prayer Focus:

Ask the Holy Spirit to fill you and produce His fruit in your life daily.

Perseverance, Service, and Long-Term Discipleship

The journey of faith continues beyond recovery. God calls us to persevere, to serve others, and to walk in long-term discipleship. By mentoring others, serving in the body of Christ, and staying faithful, we ensure that the work God has begun in us continues to bear fruit for His kingdom.

Key Scriptures:

• Hebrews 12:1–2 (NIV) *"Let us run with perseverance the race marked out for us, fixing our eyes on Jesus, the pioneer and perfecter of faith."*

• Matthew 25:21 (NIV) – *"Well done, good and faithful servant! You have been faithful with a few things; I will put you in charge of many things. Come and share your master's happiness!"*

Reflection Questions:

How can you serve others as part of your ongoing discipleship?

_____

_____

_____

What practices will help you persevere in your faith for the long term?

_____

_____

_____

Prayer Focus:

Pray for perseverance, a servant's heart, and faithfulness to walk with Christ for a lifetime.

Prayer Guide to Fight the Good Fight

(The Sword of the Spirit – Ephesians 6:17)

When temptation, fear, or destructive thoughts come, use these Scriptures as weapons of truth. Speak them out loud, declare them over your life, and remember God's promises.

When You Feel Weak or Overwhelmed

- *"My grace is sufficient for you, for My power is made perfect in weakness."* (2 Corinthians 12:9) (NIV)
- *"I can do all things through Christ who strengthens me."* (Philippians 4:13) (KJV)

When Temptation Comes

- *"No temptation has overtaken you except what is common to mankind. And God is faithful; He will not let you be tempted beyond what you can bear. But when you are tempted, He will also provide a way out so that you can endure it."* (1 Corinthians 10:13) (NIV)
- *"Submit yourselves, then, to God. Resist the devil, and he will flee from you."* (James 4:7) (NIV)

When You Feel Condemned or Ashamed

- *"Therefore, there is now no condemnation for those who are in Christ Jesus."* (Romans 8:1) (NIV)
- *"As far as the east is from the west, so far has He removed our transgressions from us."* (Psalm 103:12) (NIV)

When You Are Afraid

- *"For God has not given us a spirit of fear, but of power and of love and of a sound mind."* (2 Timothy 1:7) (KJV)
- *"When I am afraid, I put my trust in You."* (Psalm 56:3) (NIV)

When You Need Peace

- *"You will keep in perfect peace those whose minds are steadfast, because they trust in You."* (Isaiah 26:3) (NIV)
- *"And the peace of God, which transcends all understanding, will guard your hearts and your minds in Christ Jesus." (Philippians 4:7) (NIV)*

When You Have Trouble Sleeping or Having Nightmares

When thou liest down, thou shalt not be afraid: Yea, thou shalt lie down, and thy sleep shall be sweet. (Proverbs 3:24) (KJV)